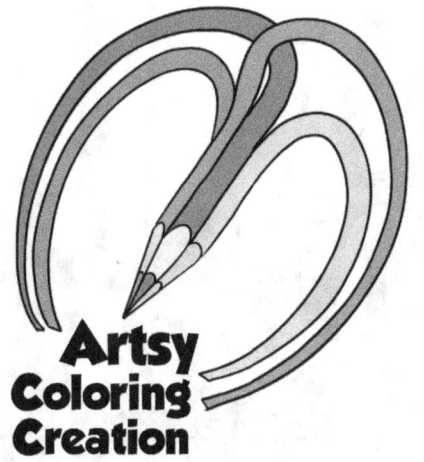

Artsy Coloring Creation

An Inspirational Coloring
Dare To Dream The Unthinkable

A coloring book featuring 50 unique inspirational quotes. Discover each design with your own coloring style. Relax, exhale, and enjoying the meaningful coloring activity.

@Artsy_coloringcreation

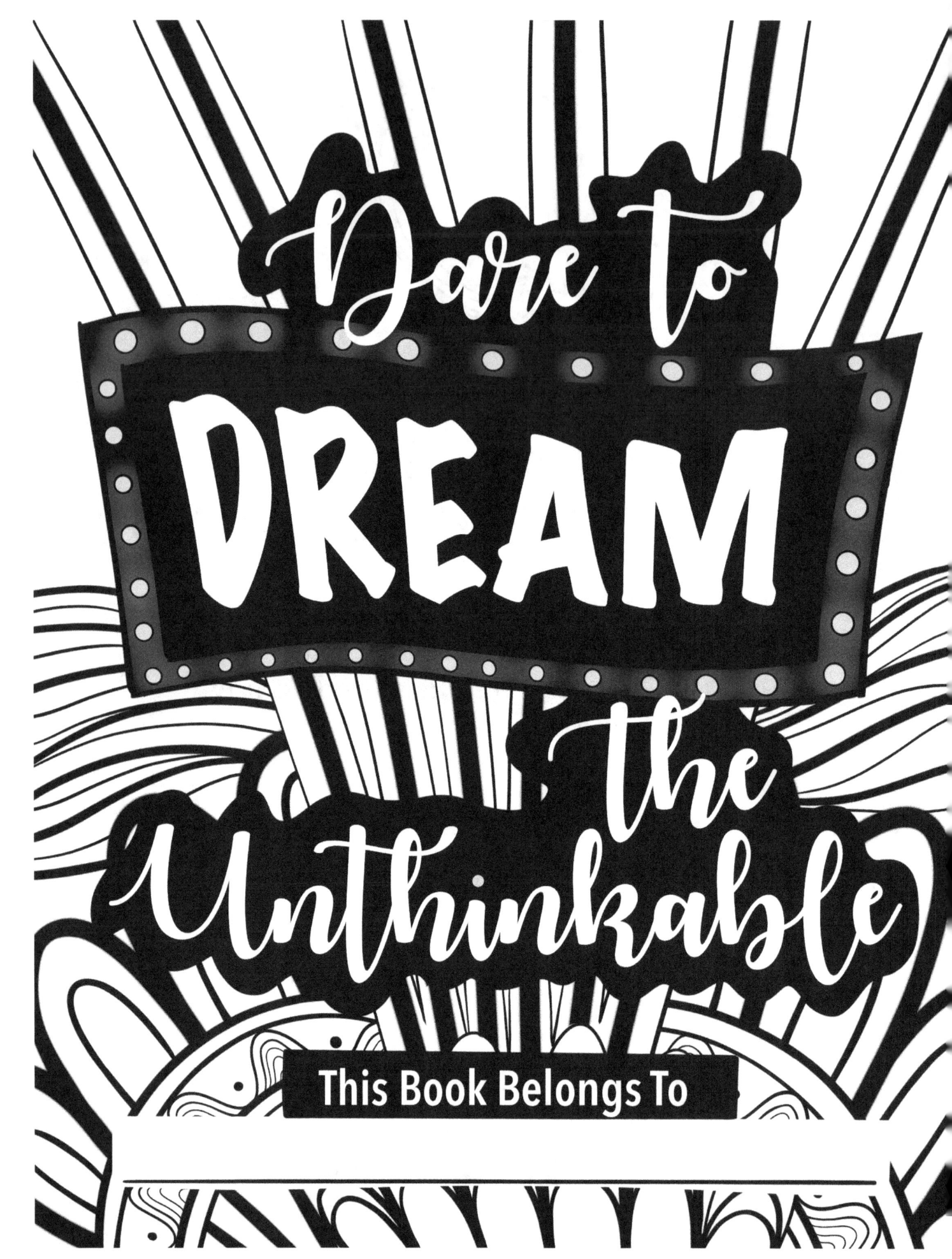

Dare to DREAM the Unthinkable

This Book Belongs To

Coloring Palette

ABOUT THE CREATOR

We are here to produce coloring contents for you to add colors into your life. Here at Artsy Coloring Creation, we are focused into creating imaginative coloring contents to take you out of reality. Passionate in drawing, we hope to bring you more content that all ages can enjoy!

DARE TO DREAM

Dream the unthinkable, do the impossible, immerse yourself in the world of inspirational and aspiration words. Color them and take time to relax. You can frame them up after you have colored your beautiful pieces.

Ready? Let's Start!

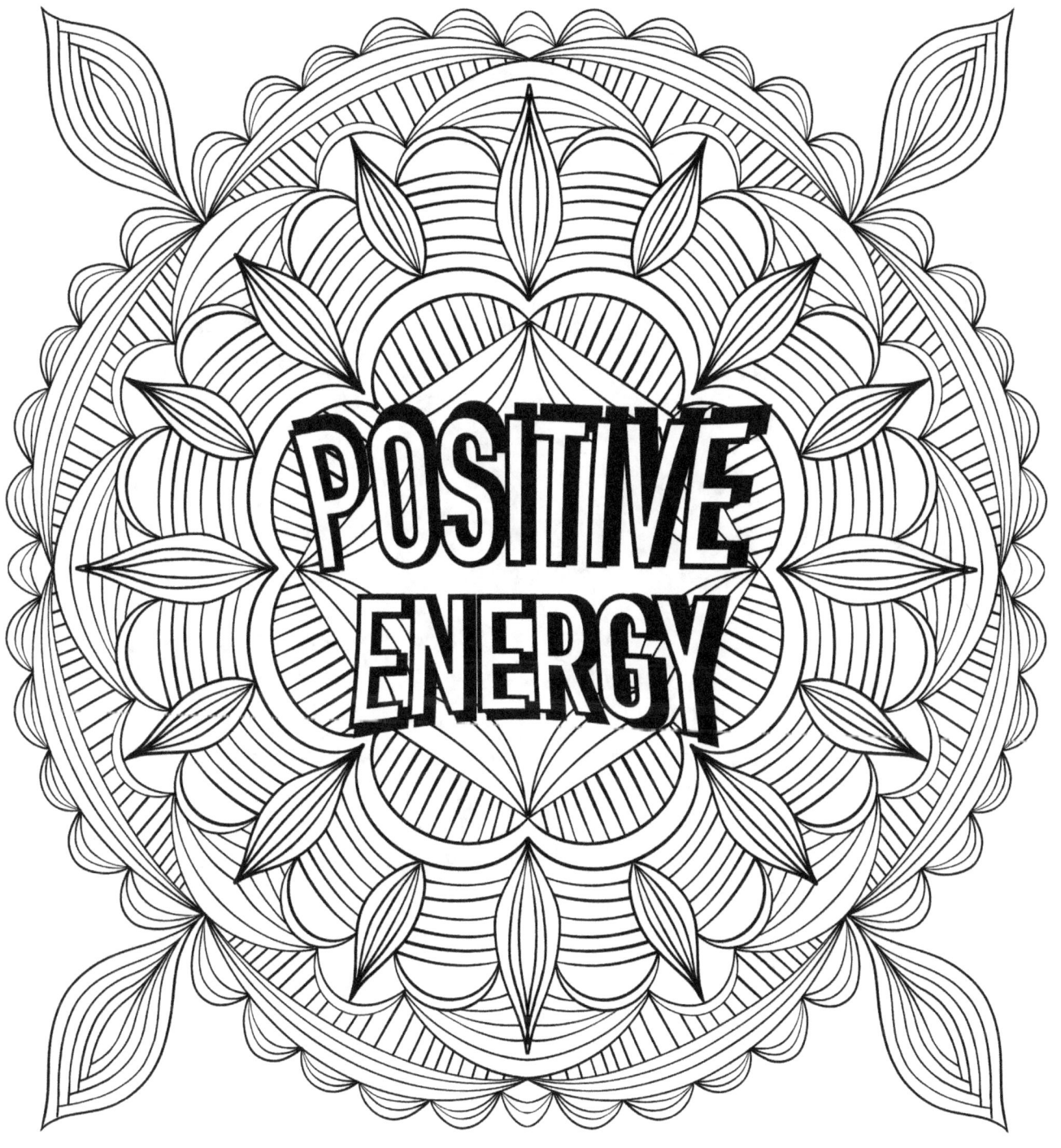

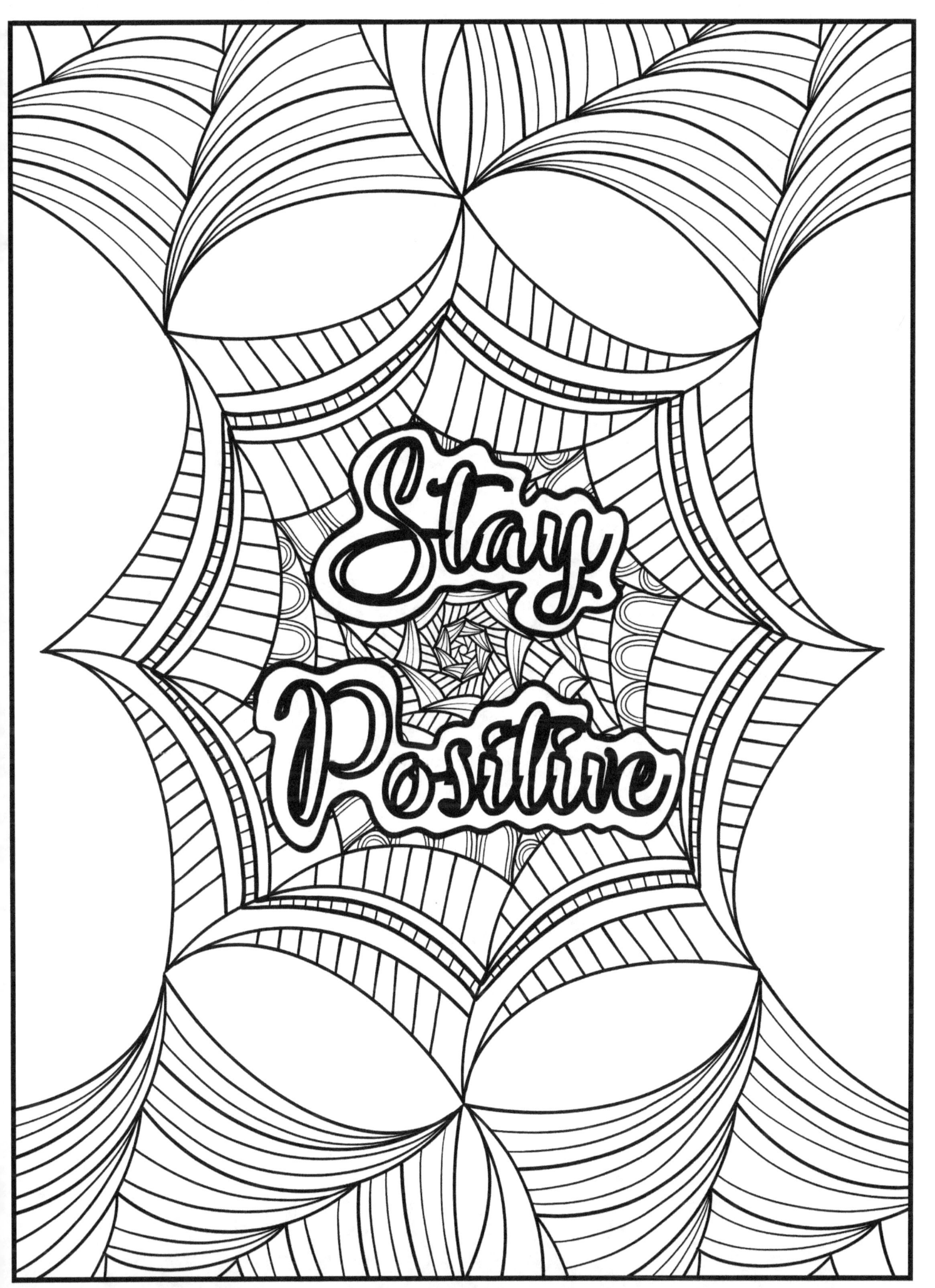

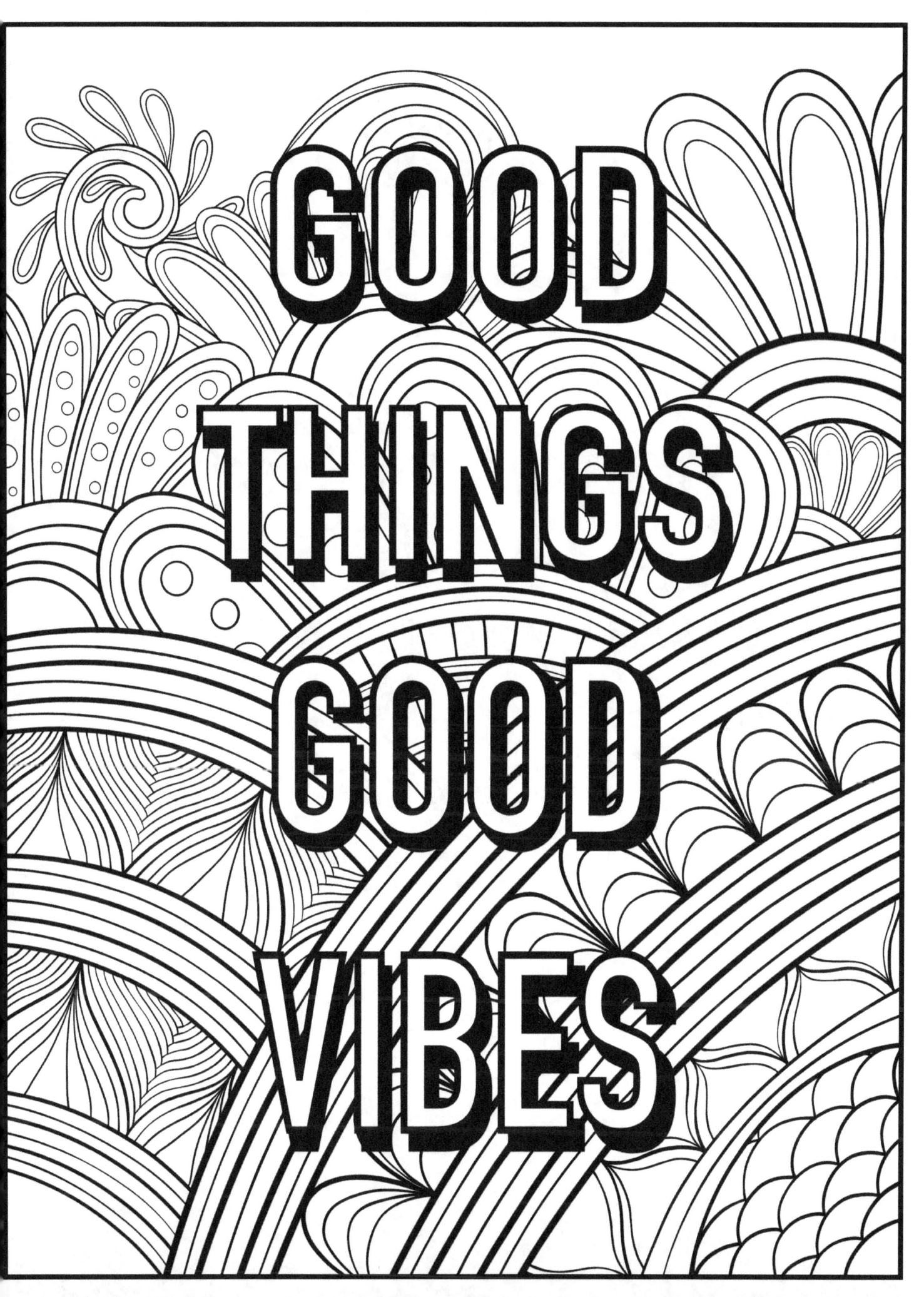

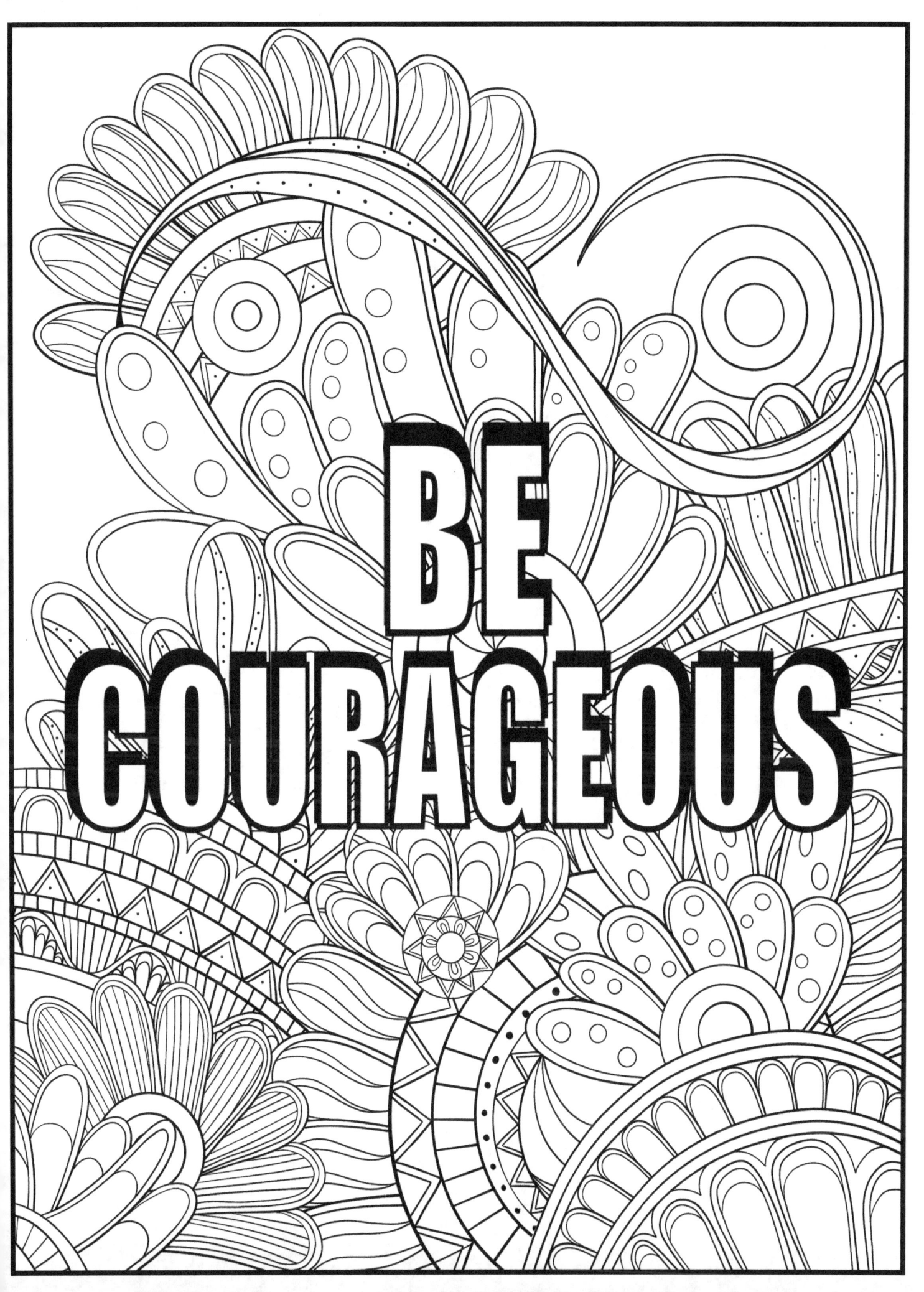

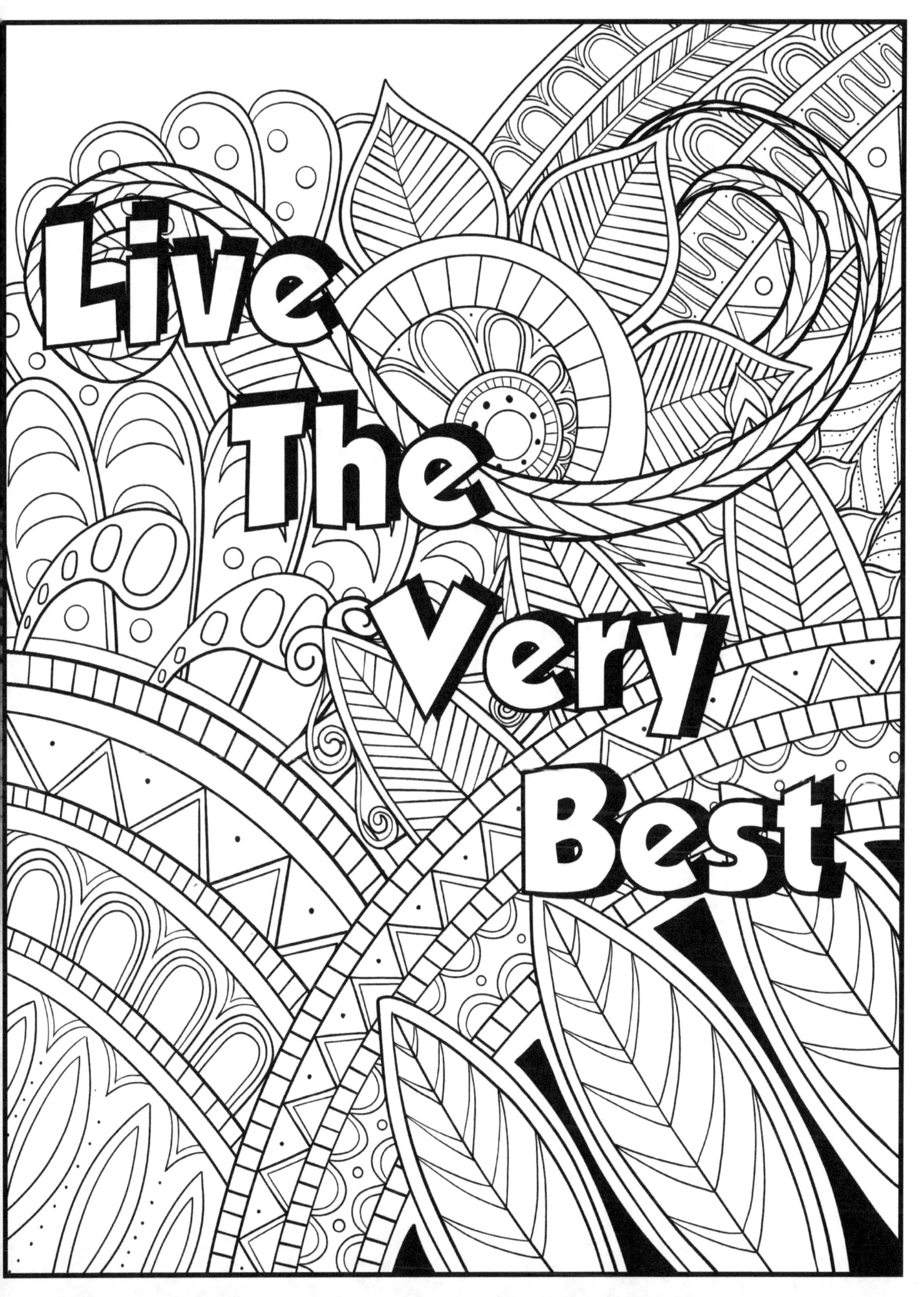

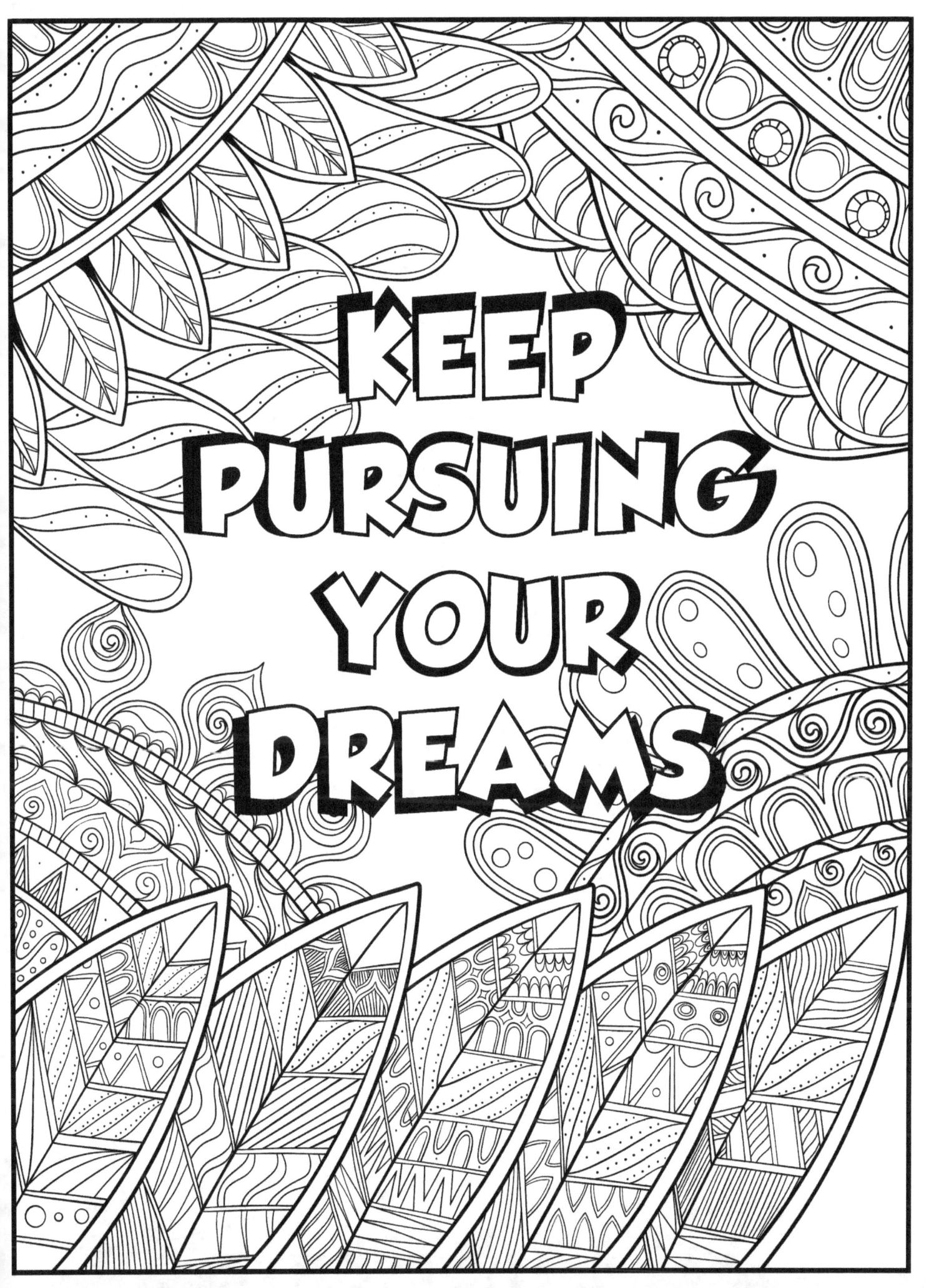

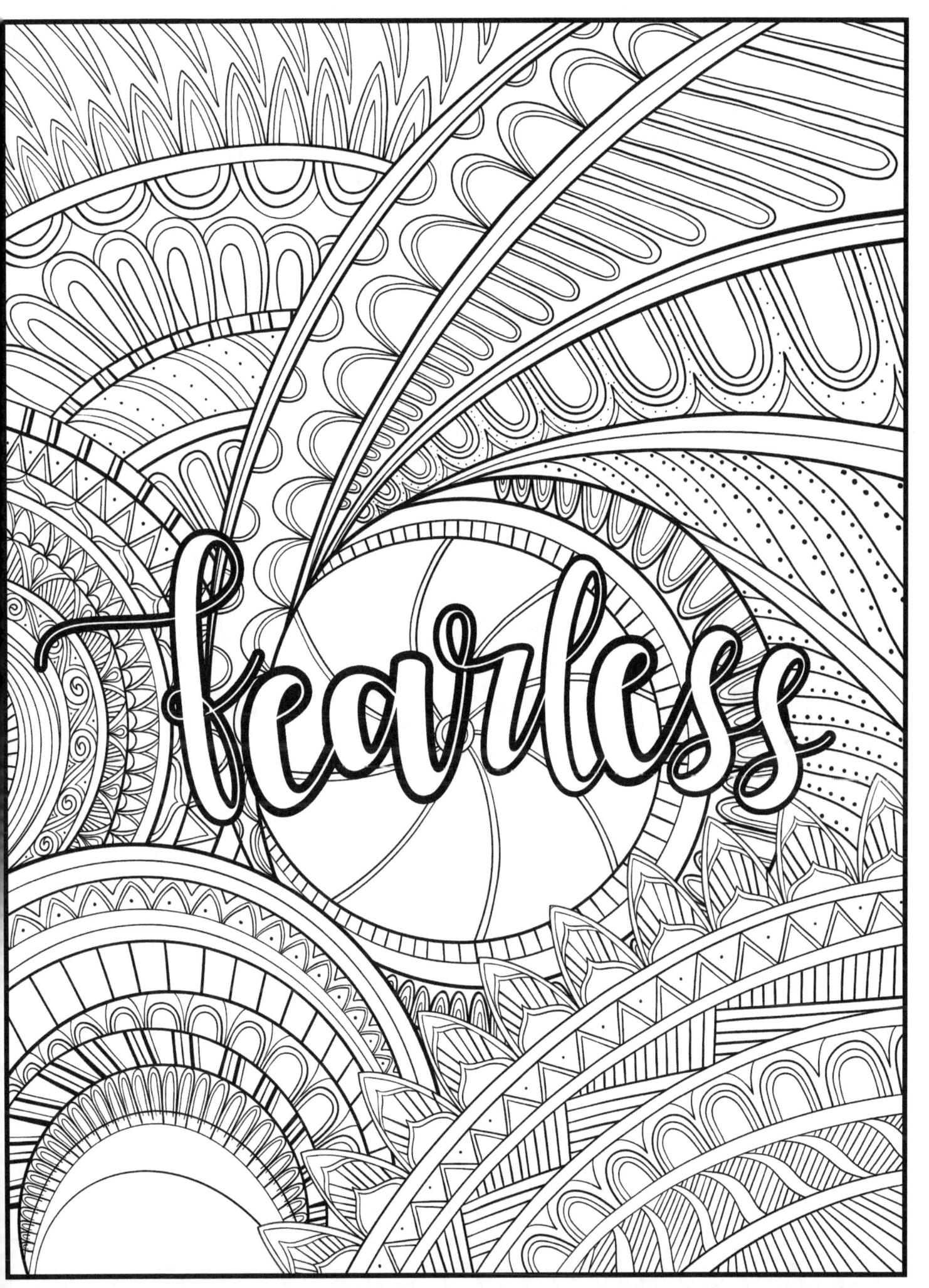

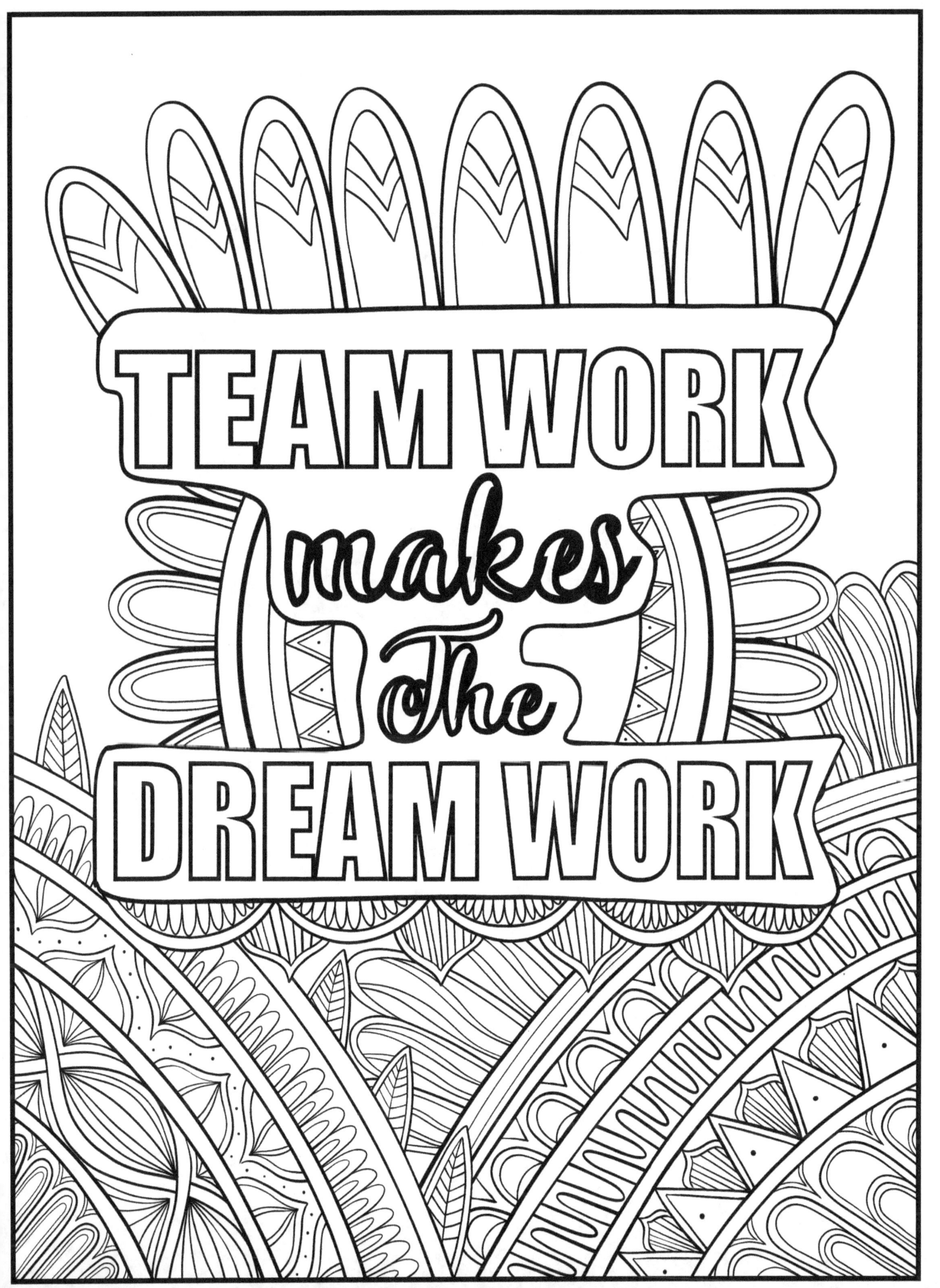

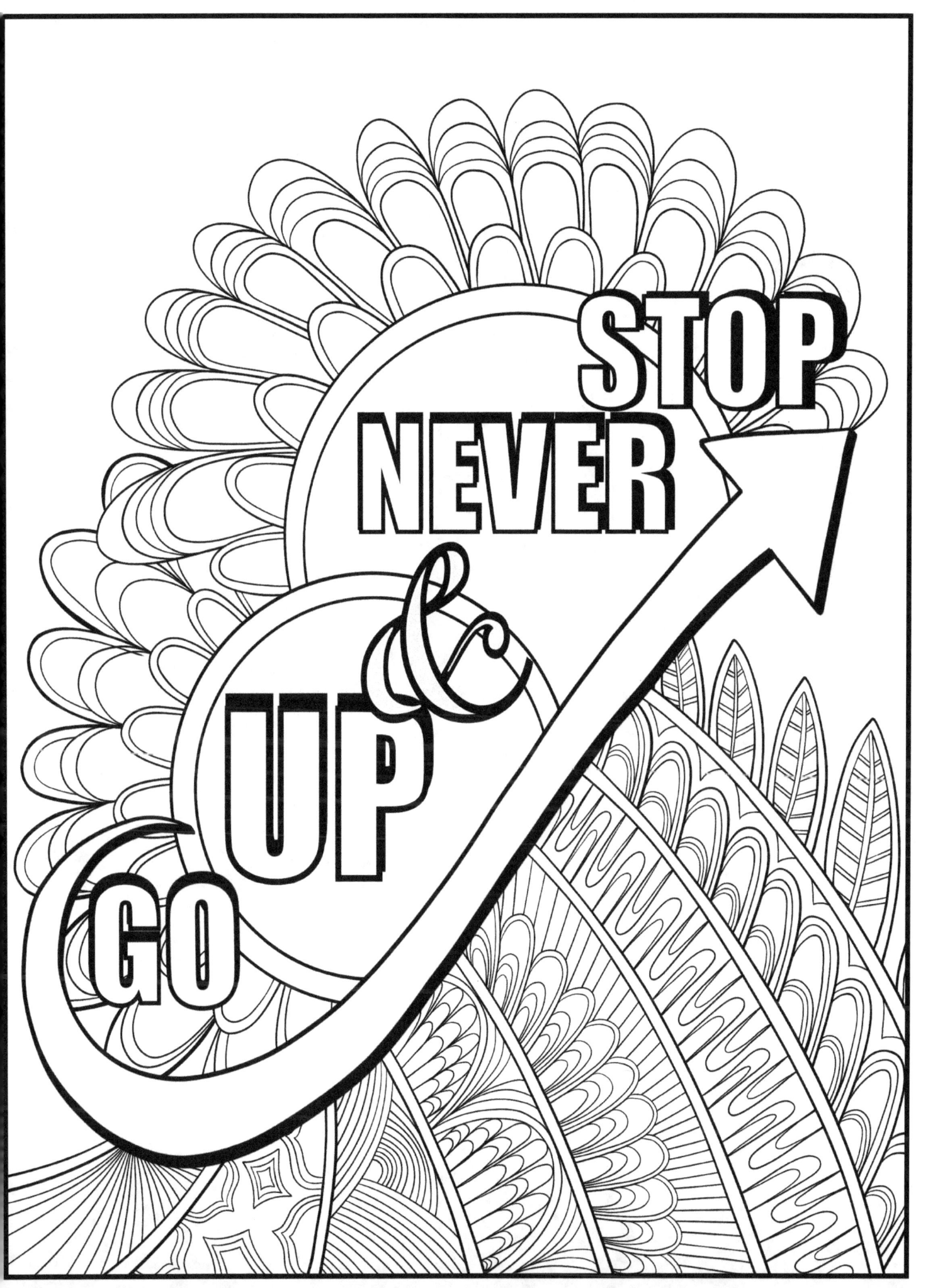

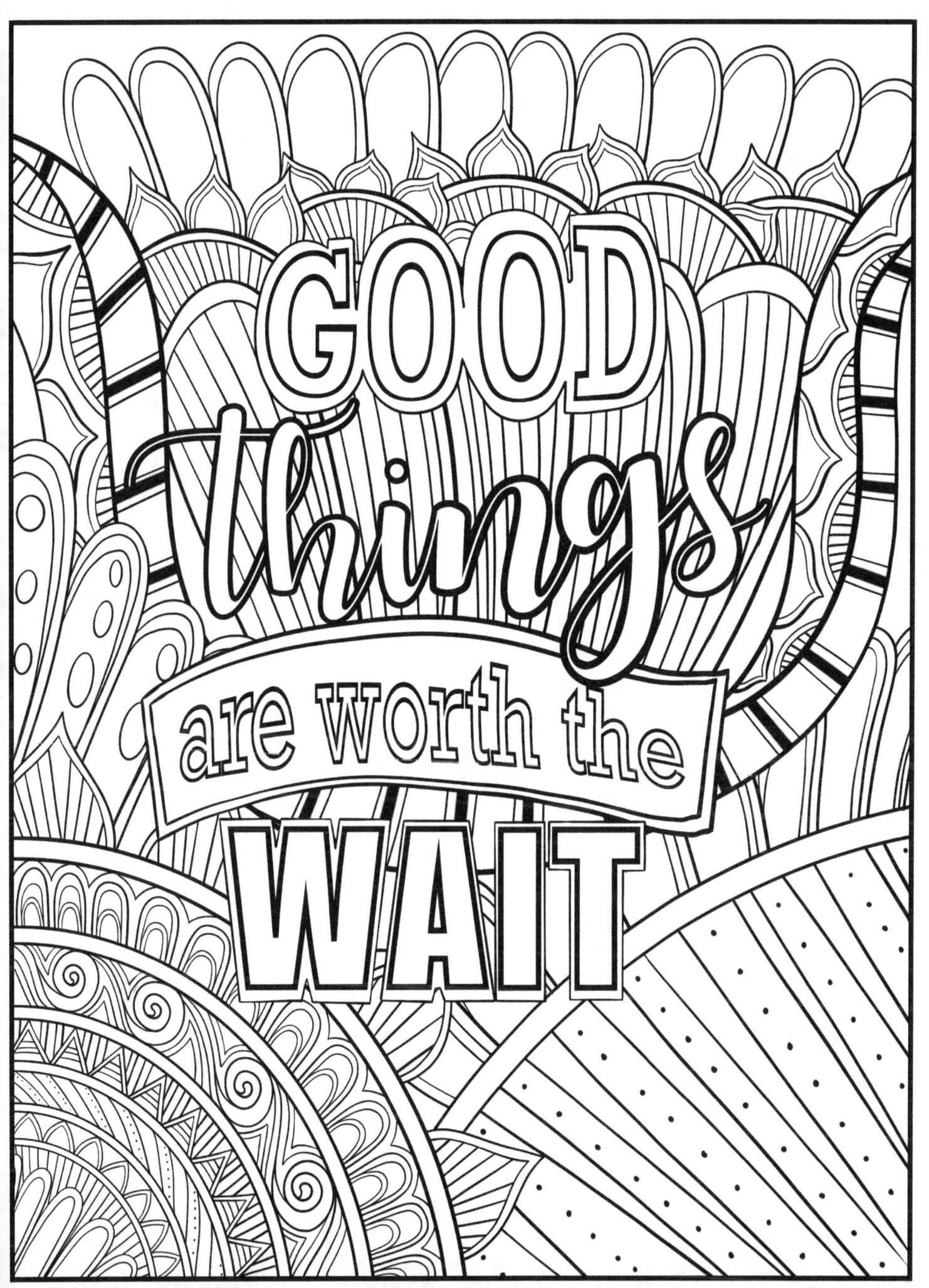

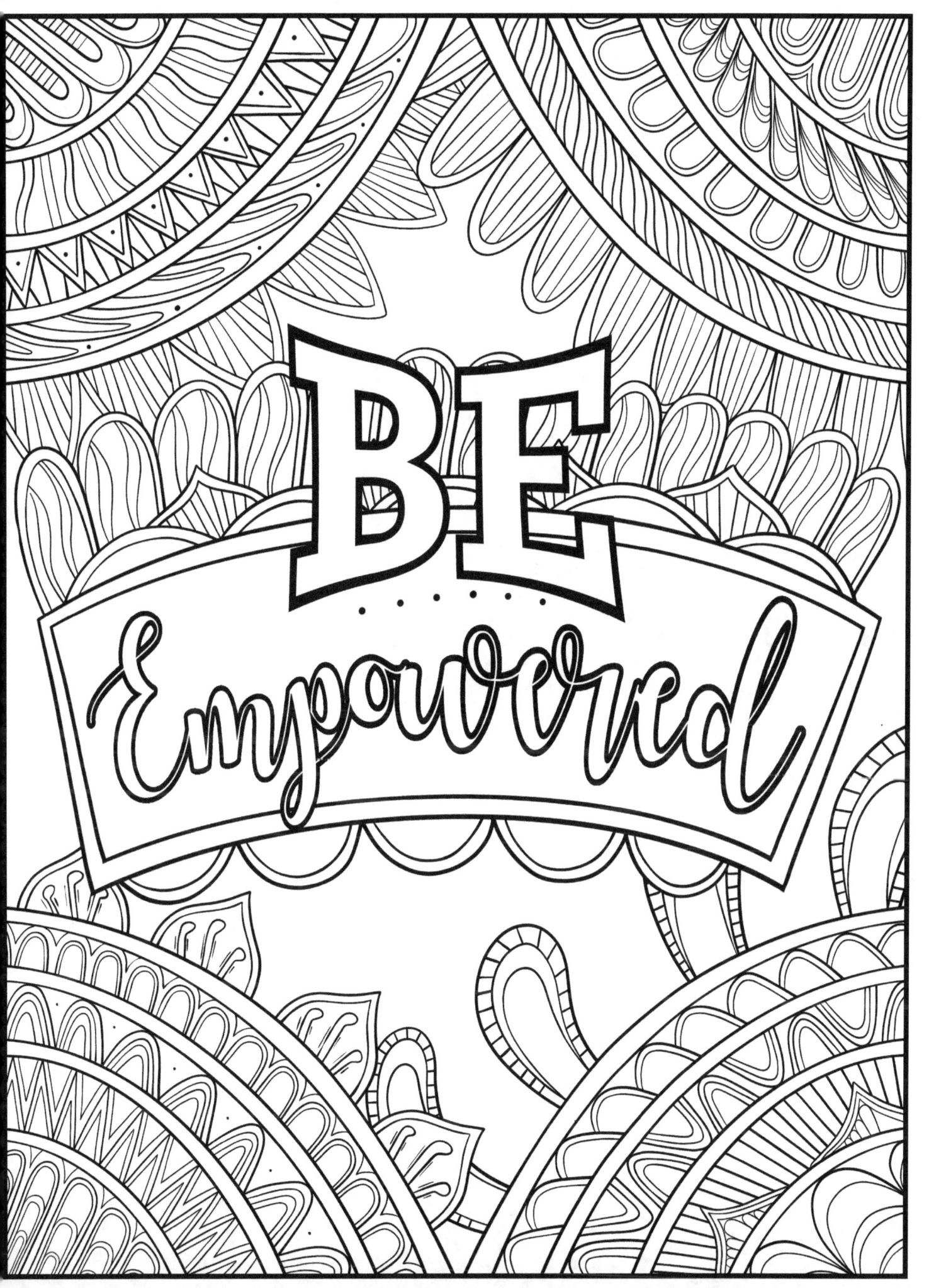

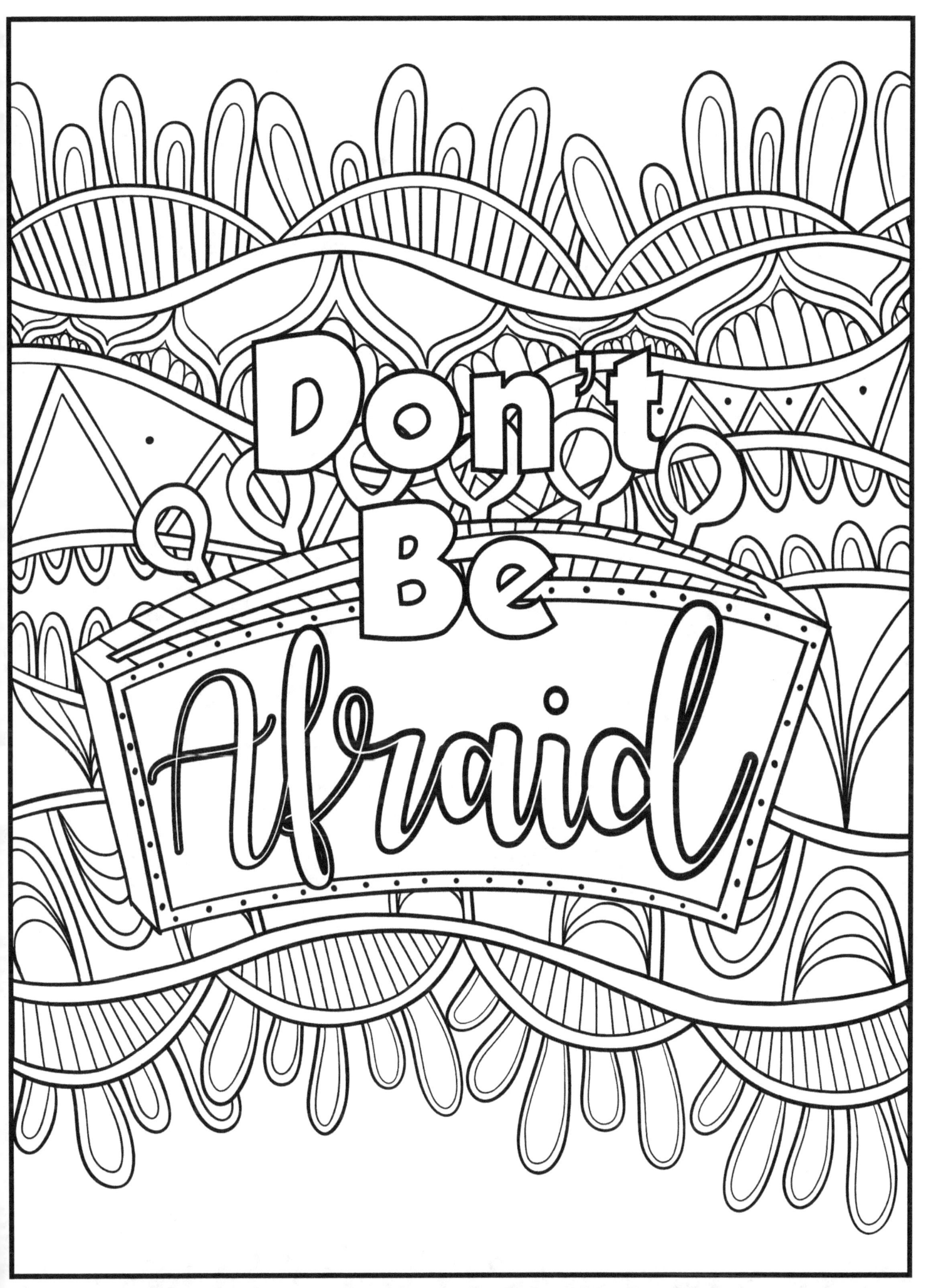

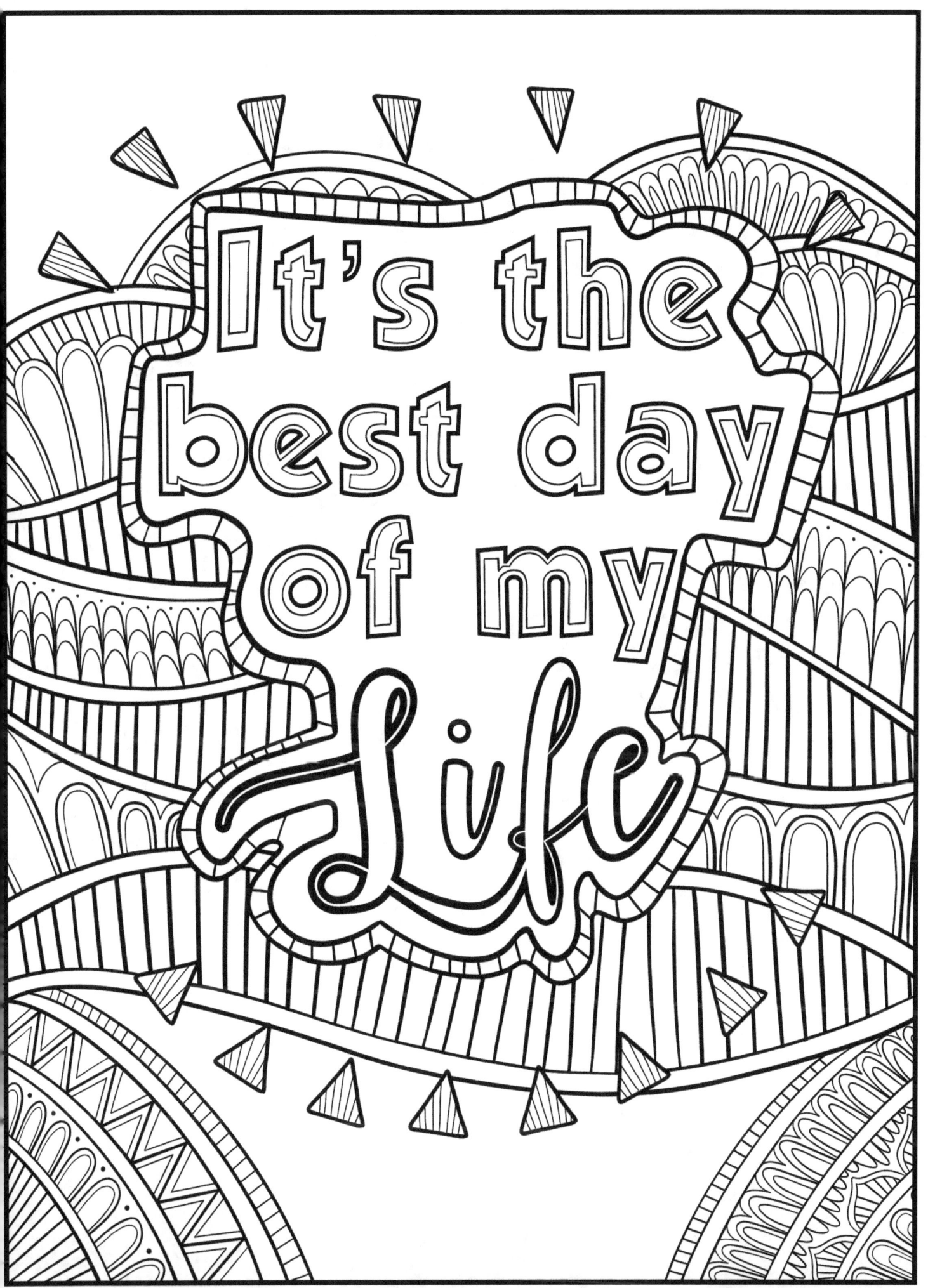

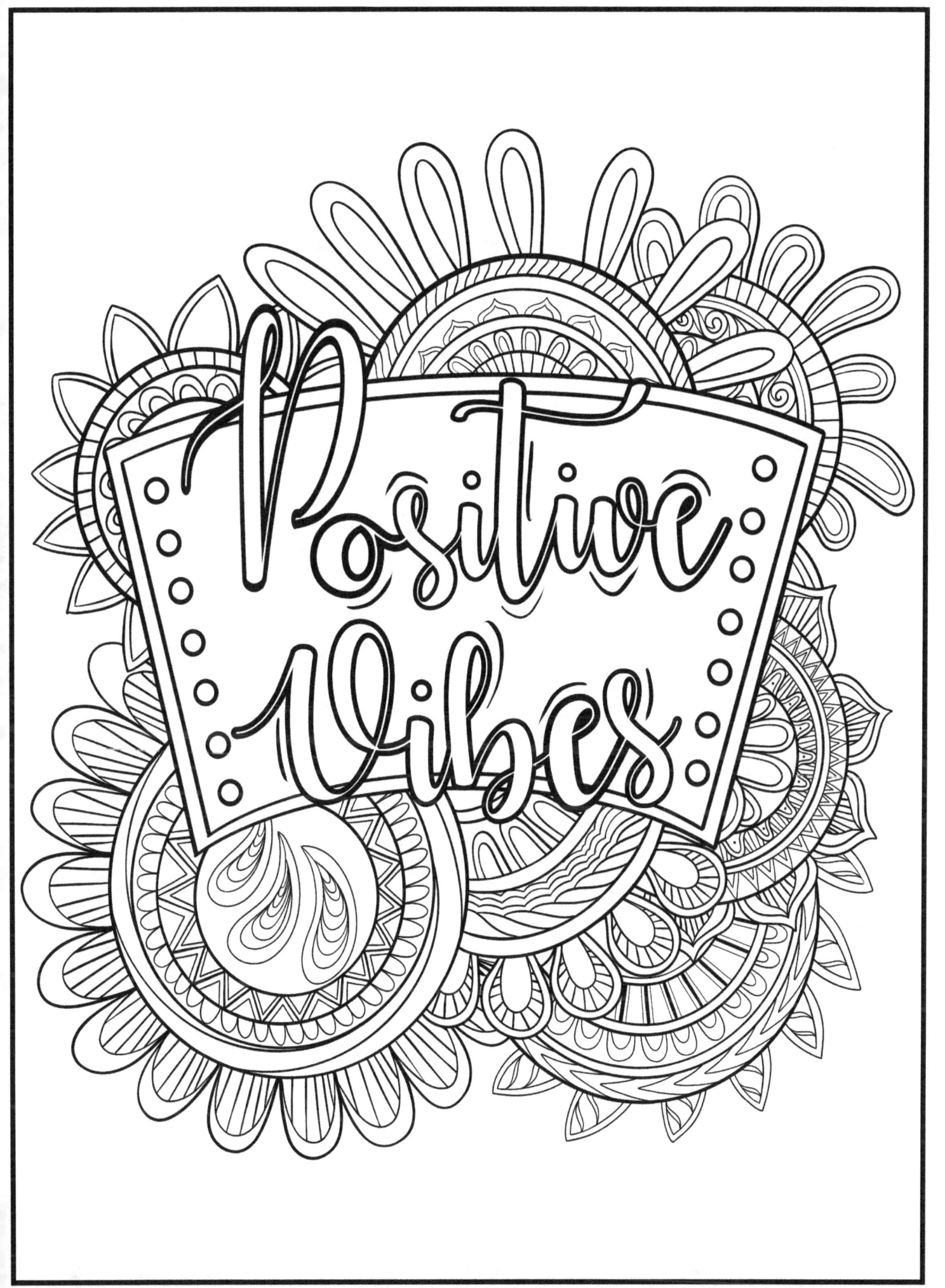

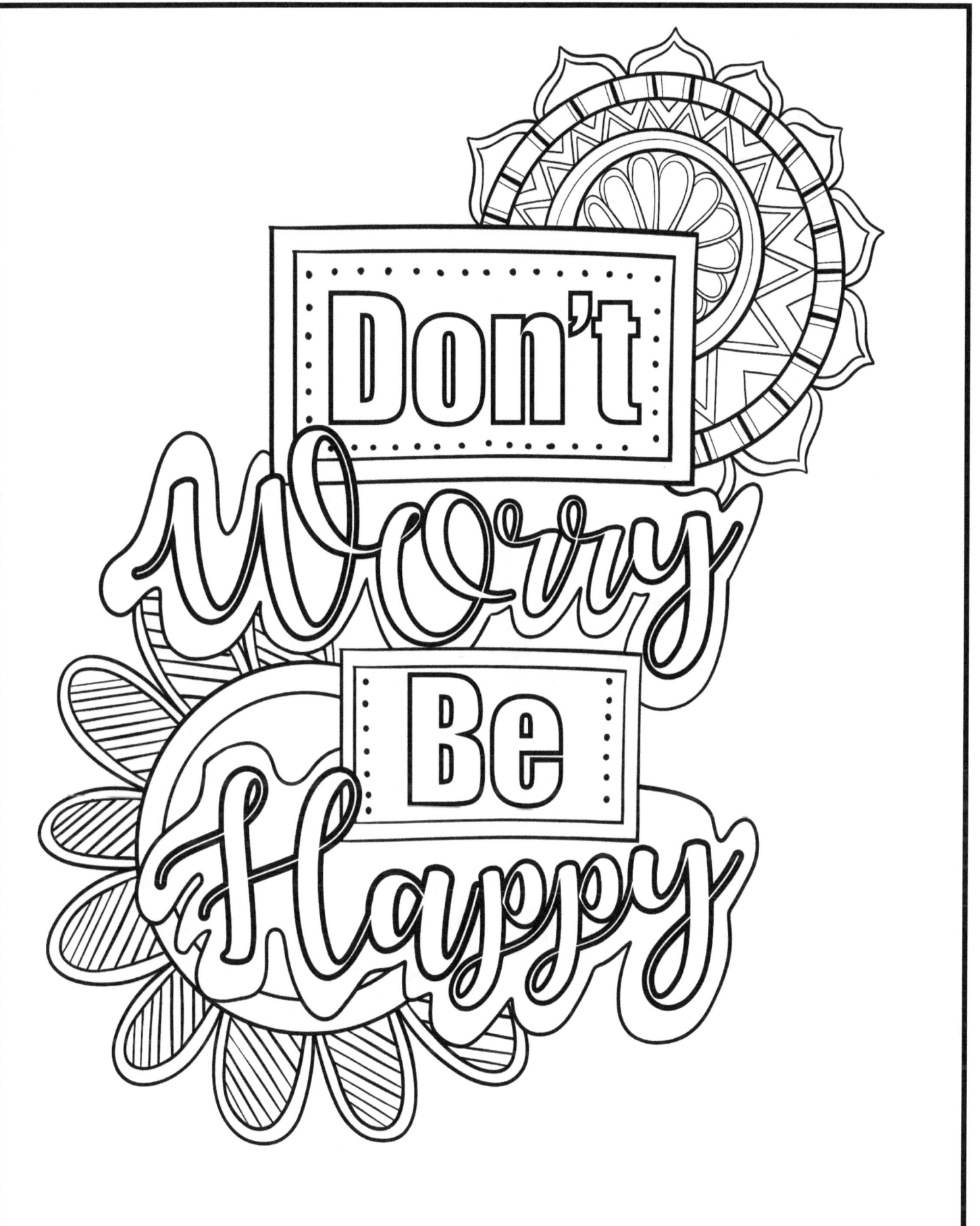

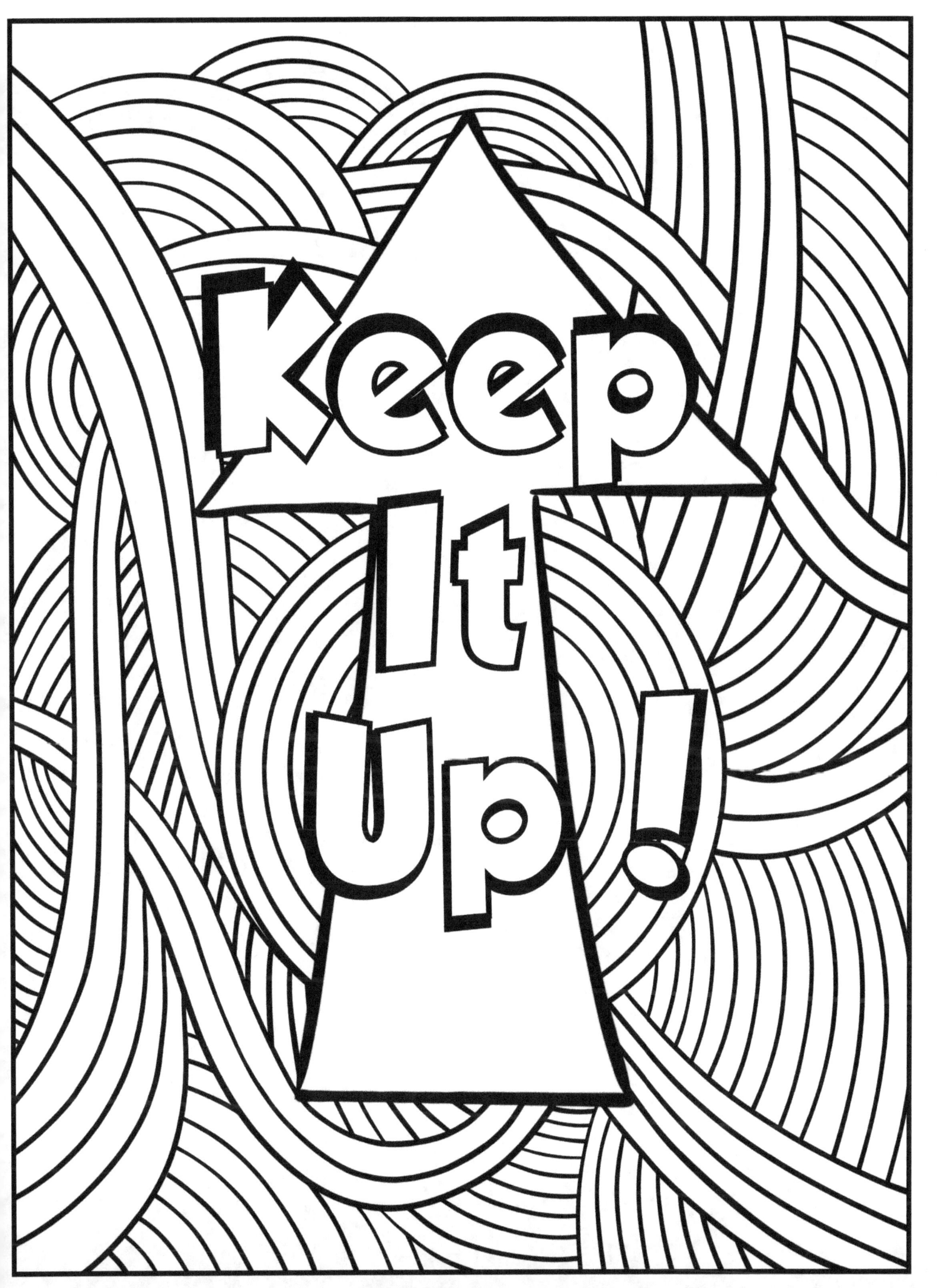

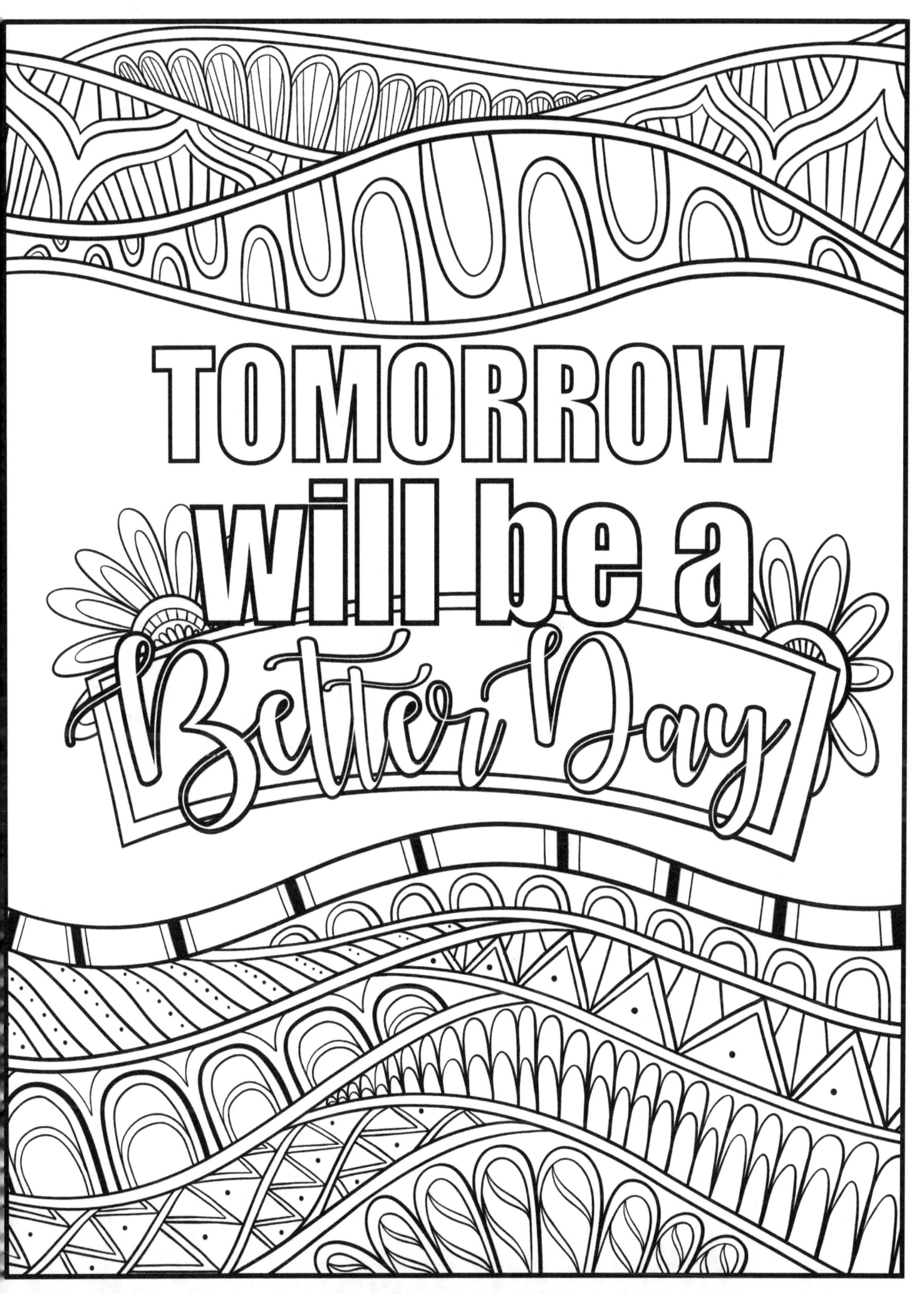

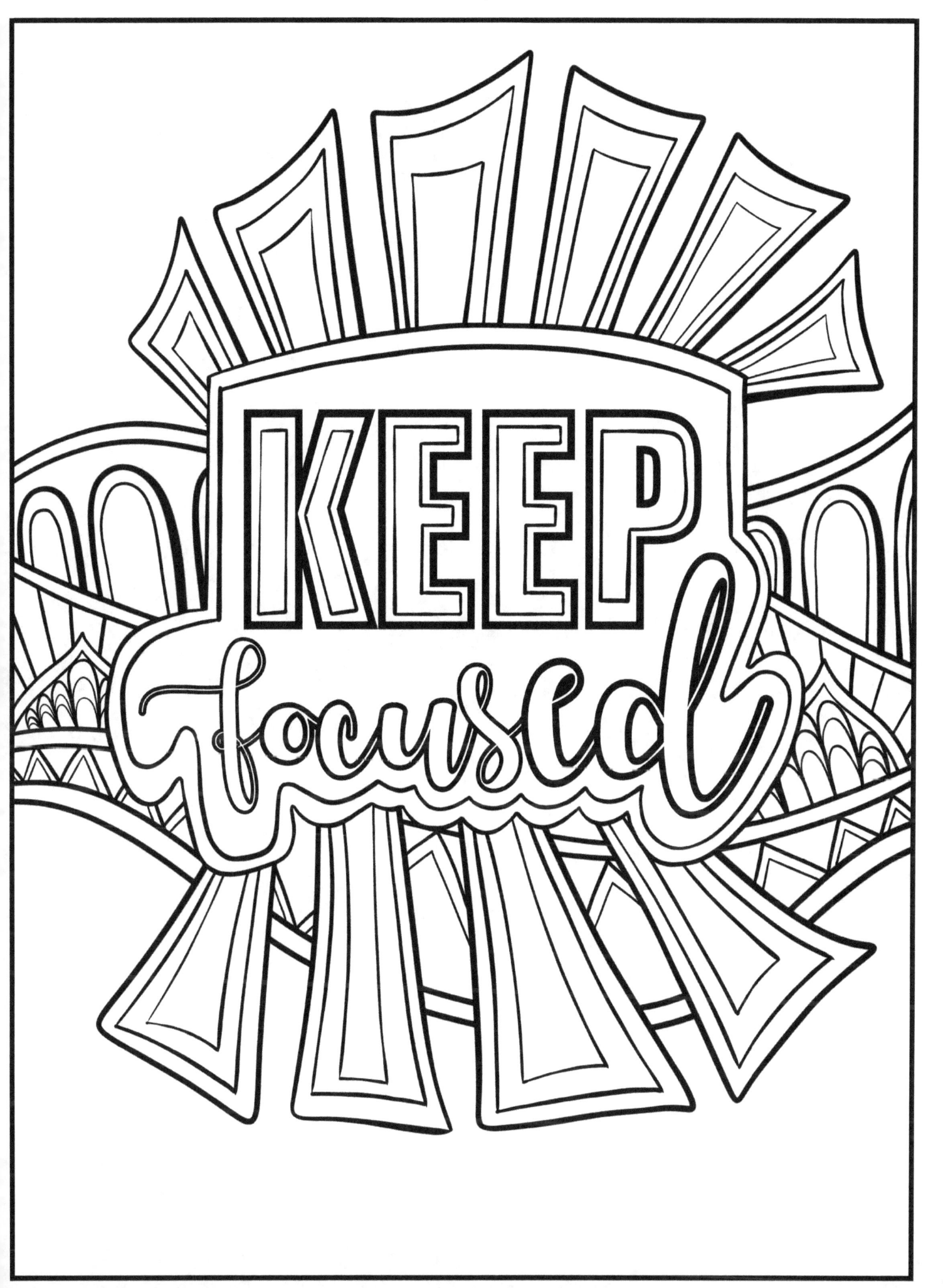

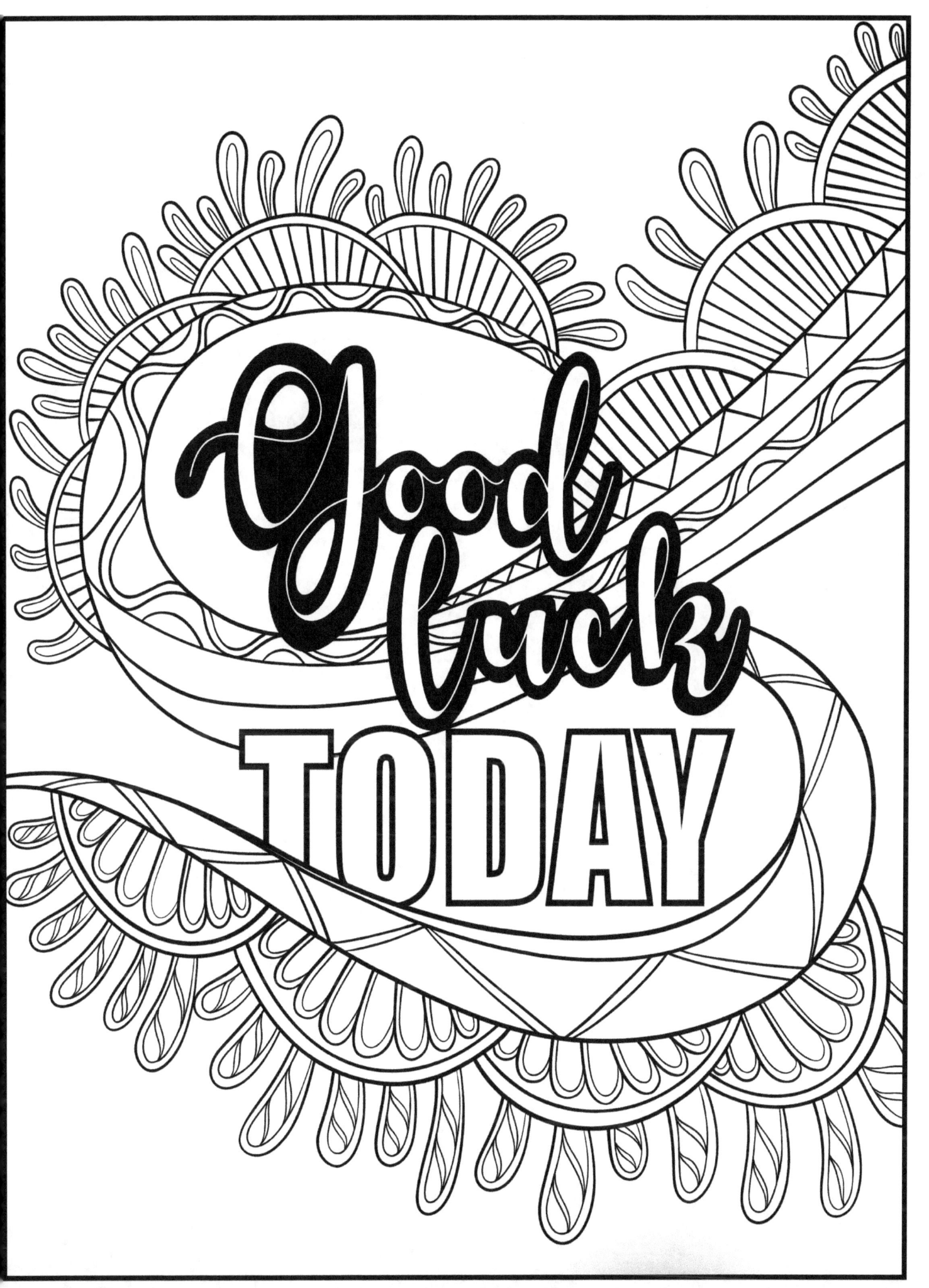

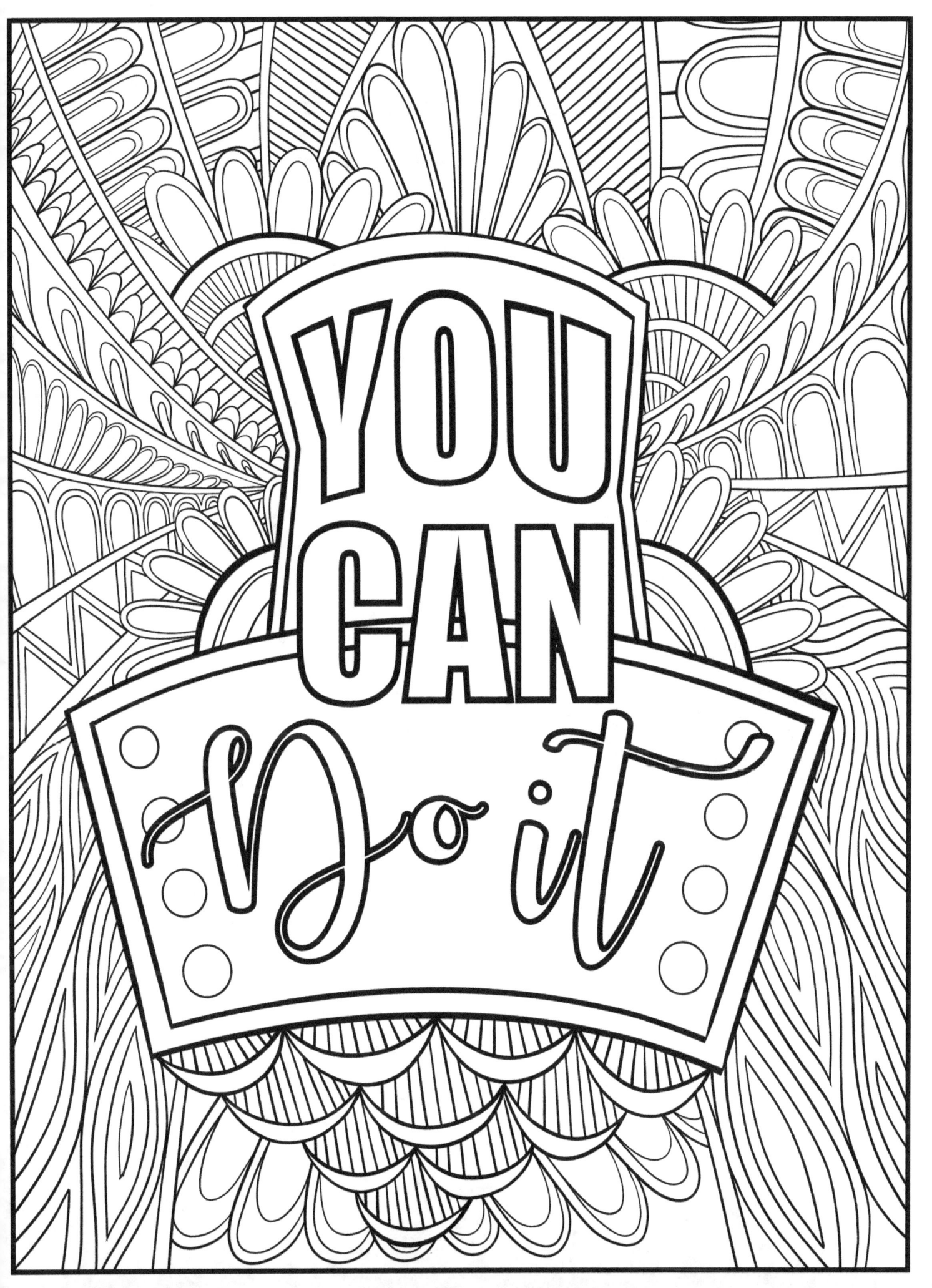

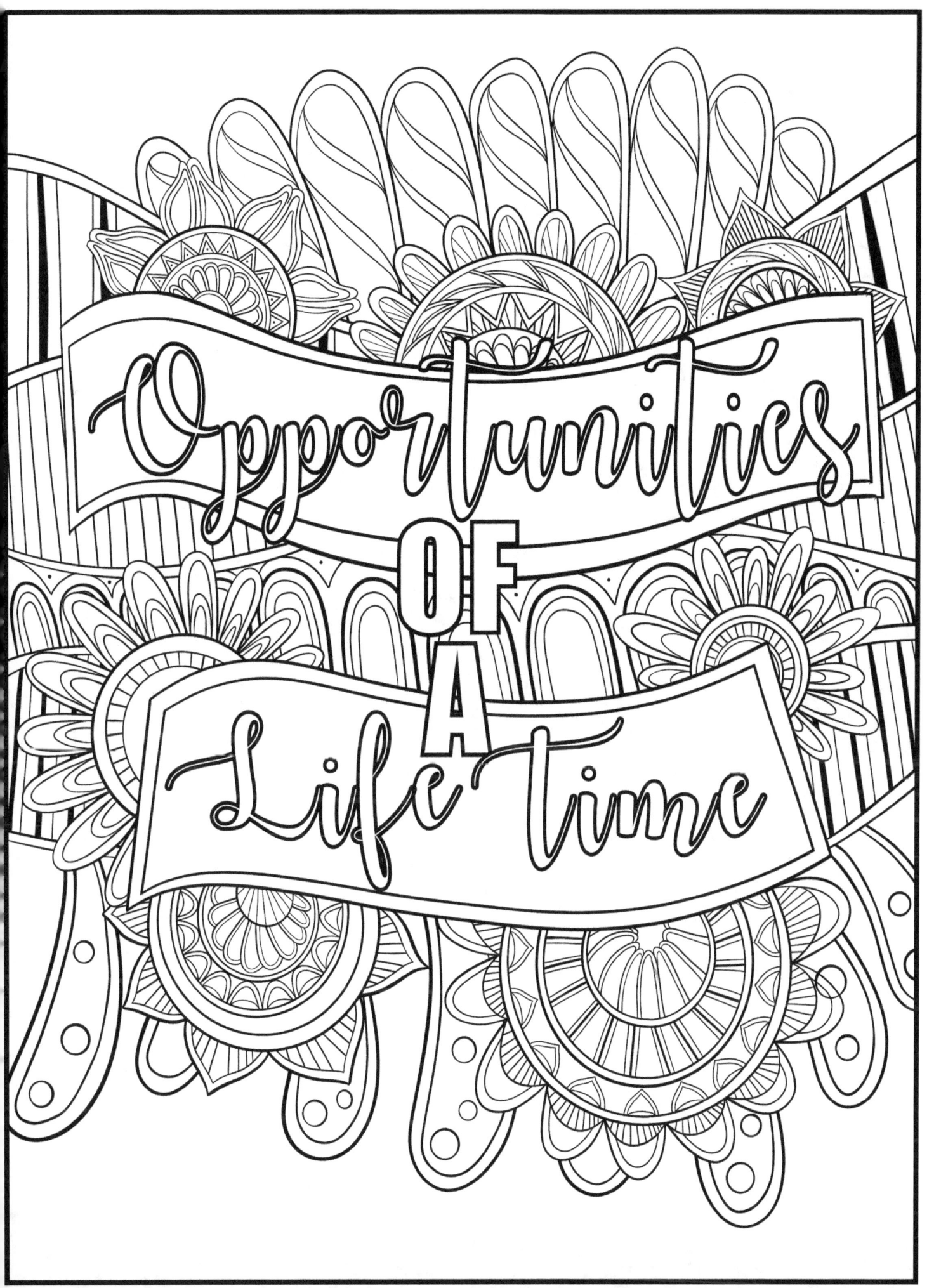

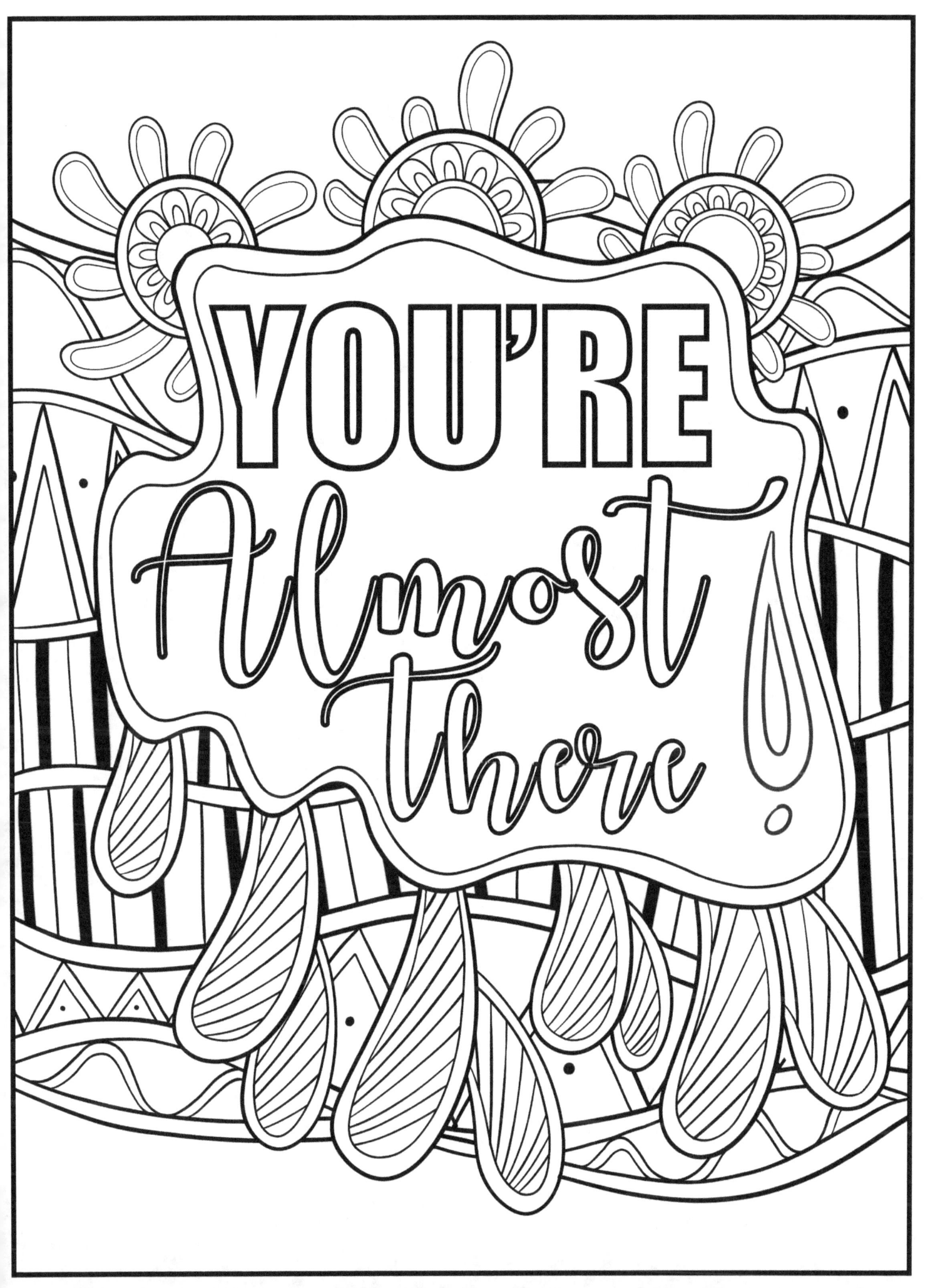

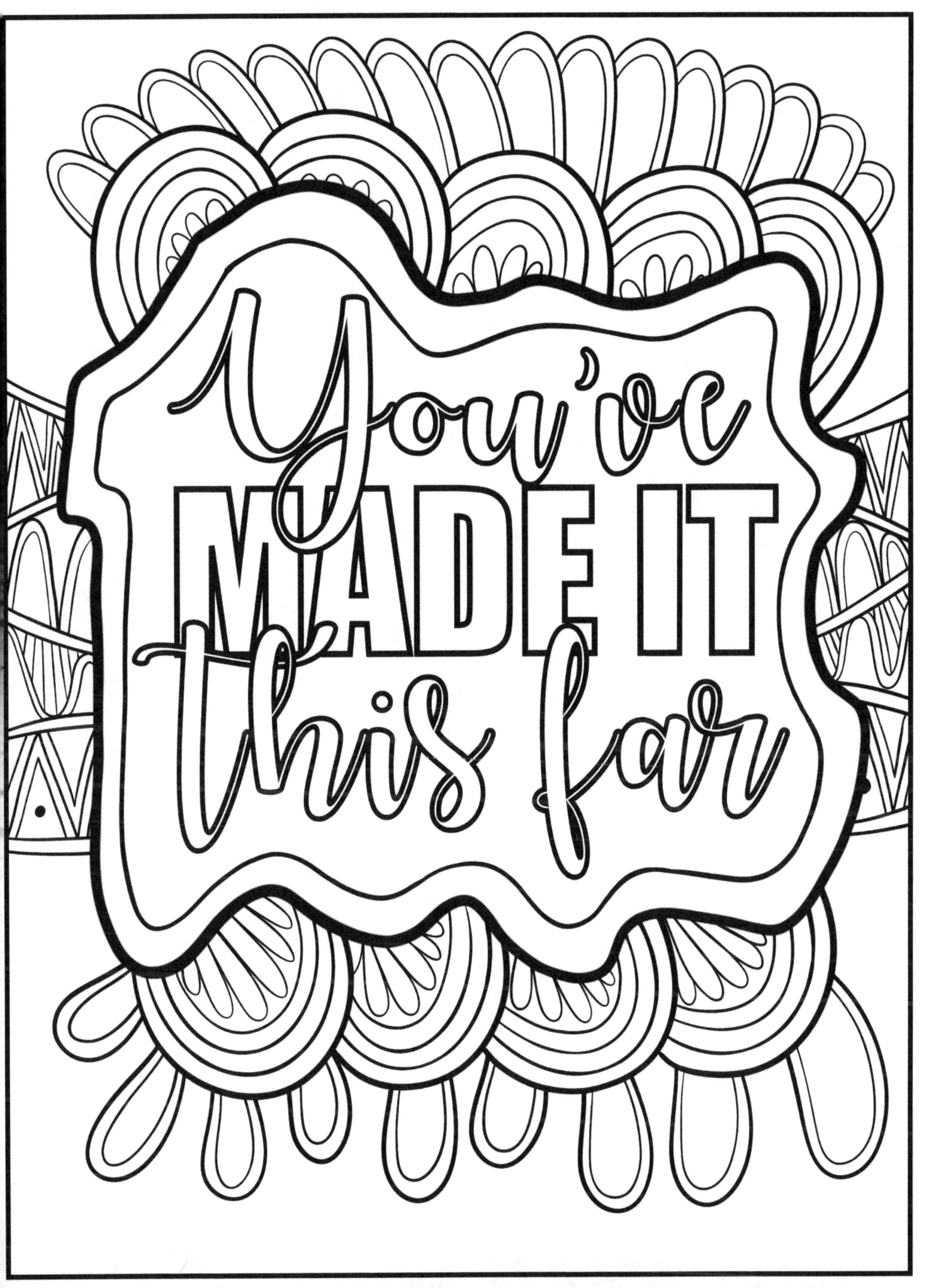

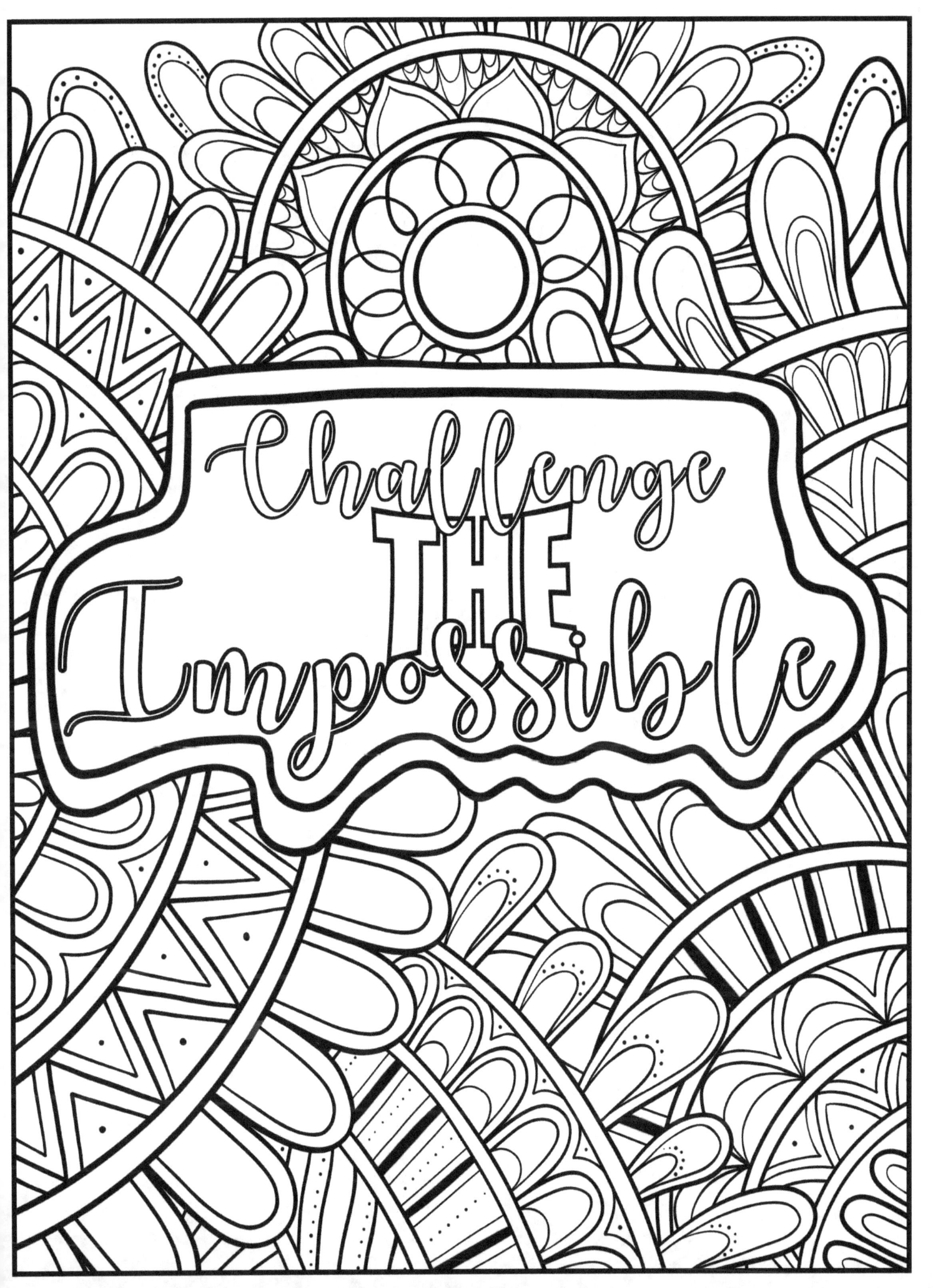

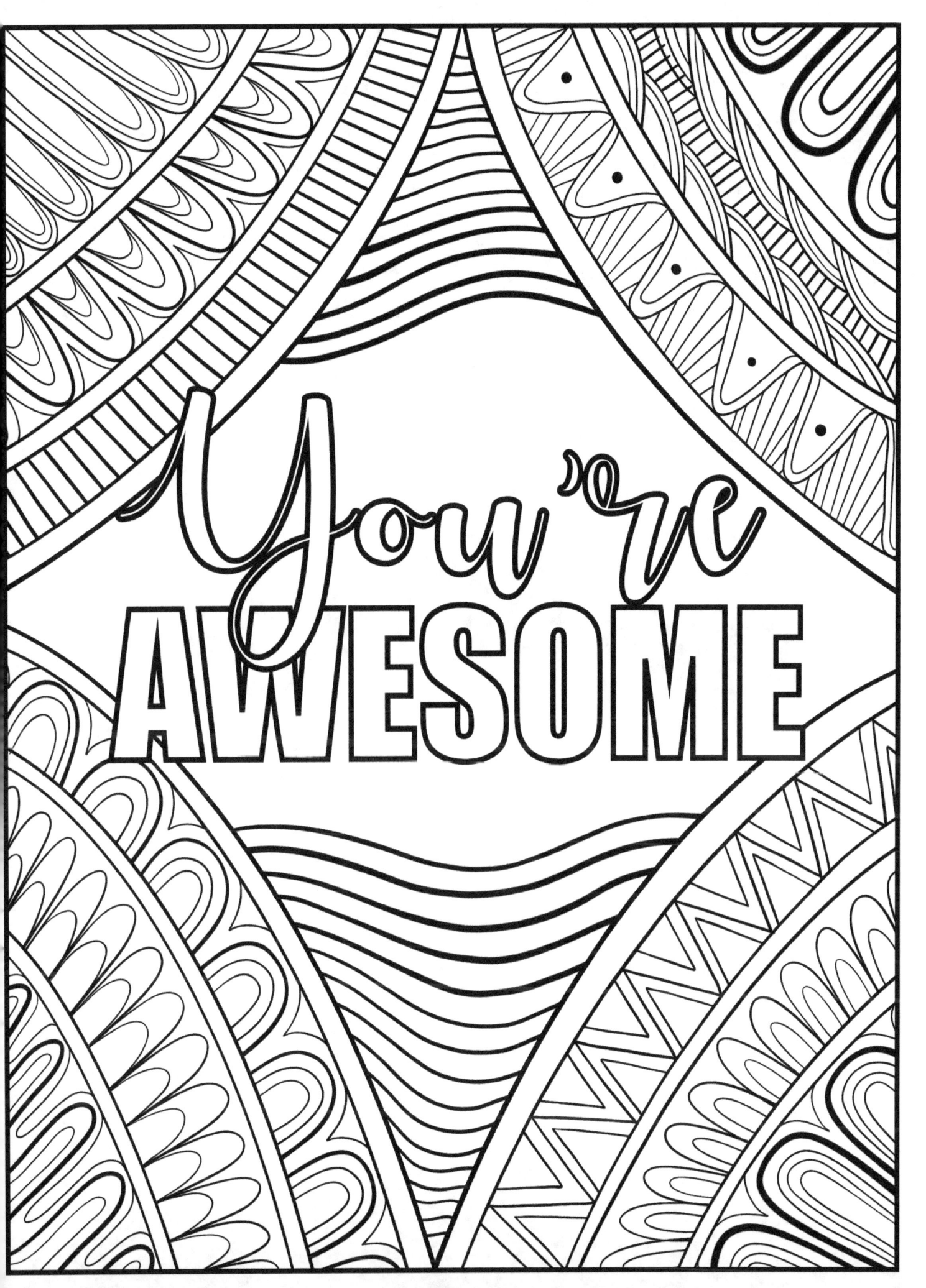

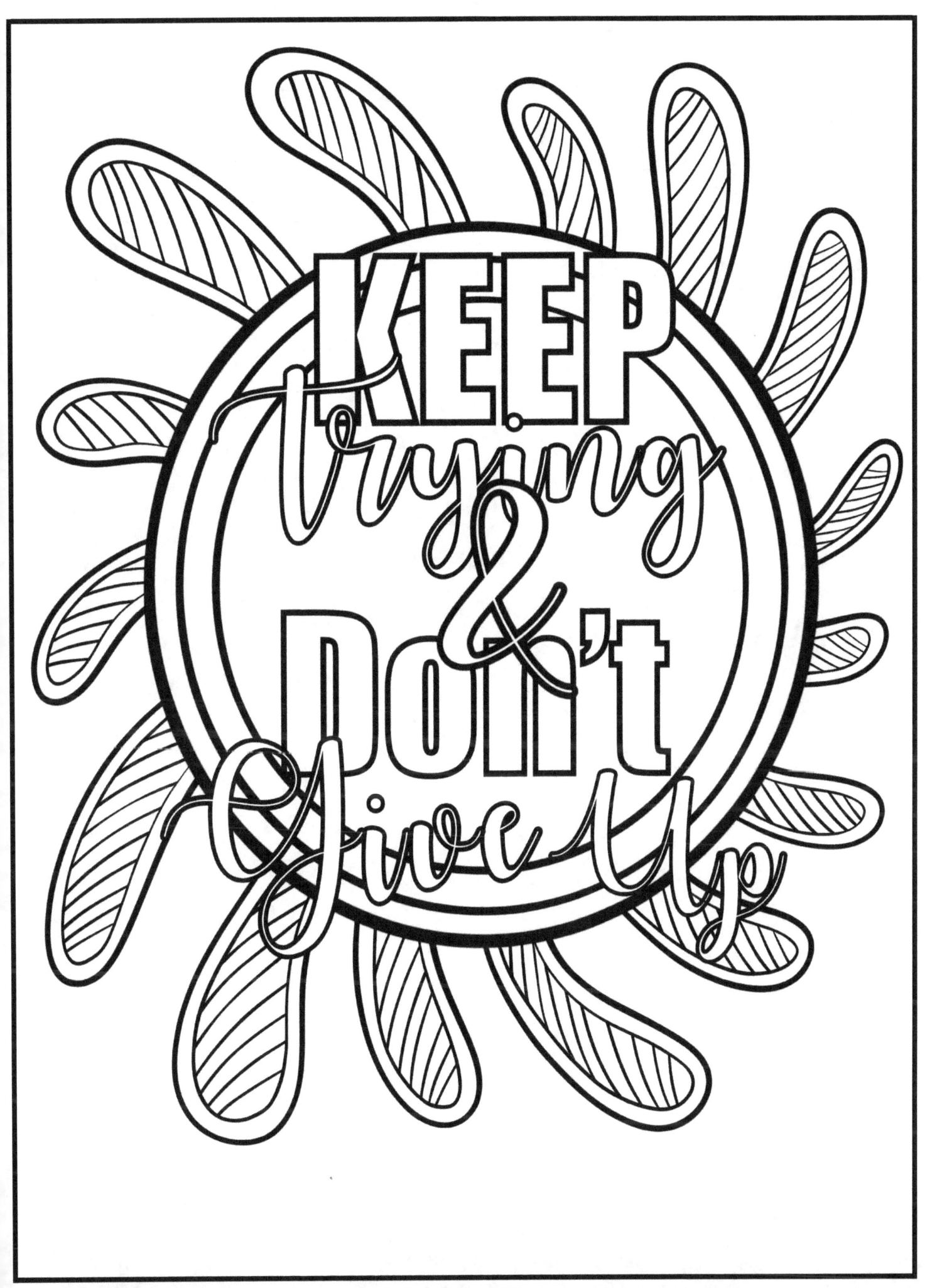

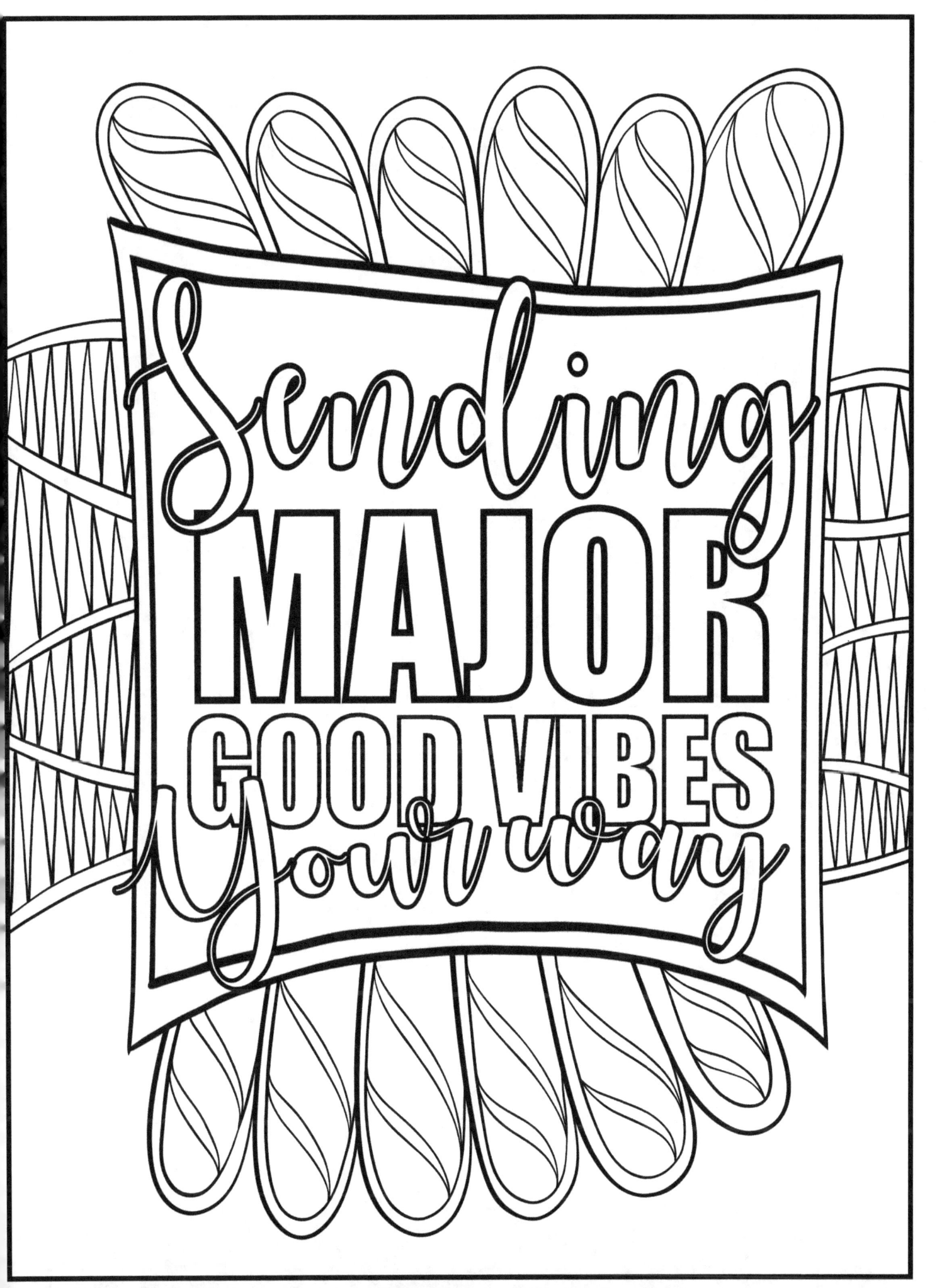

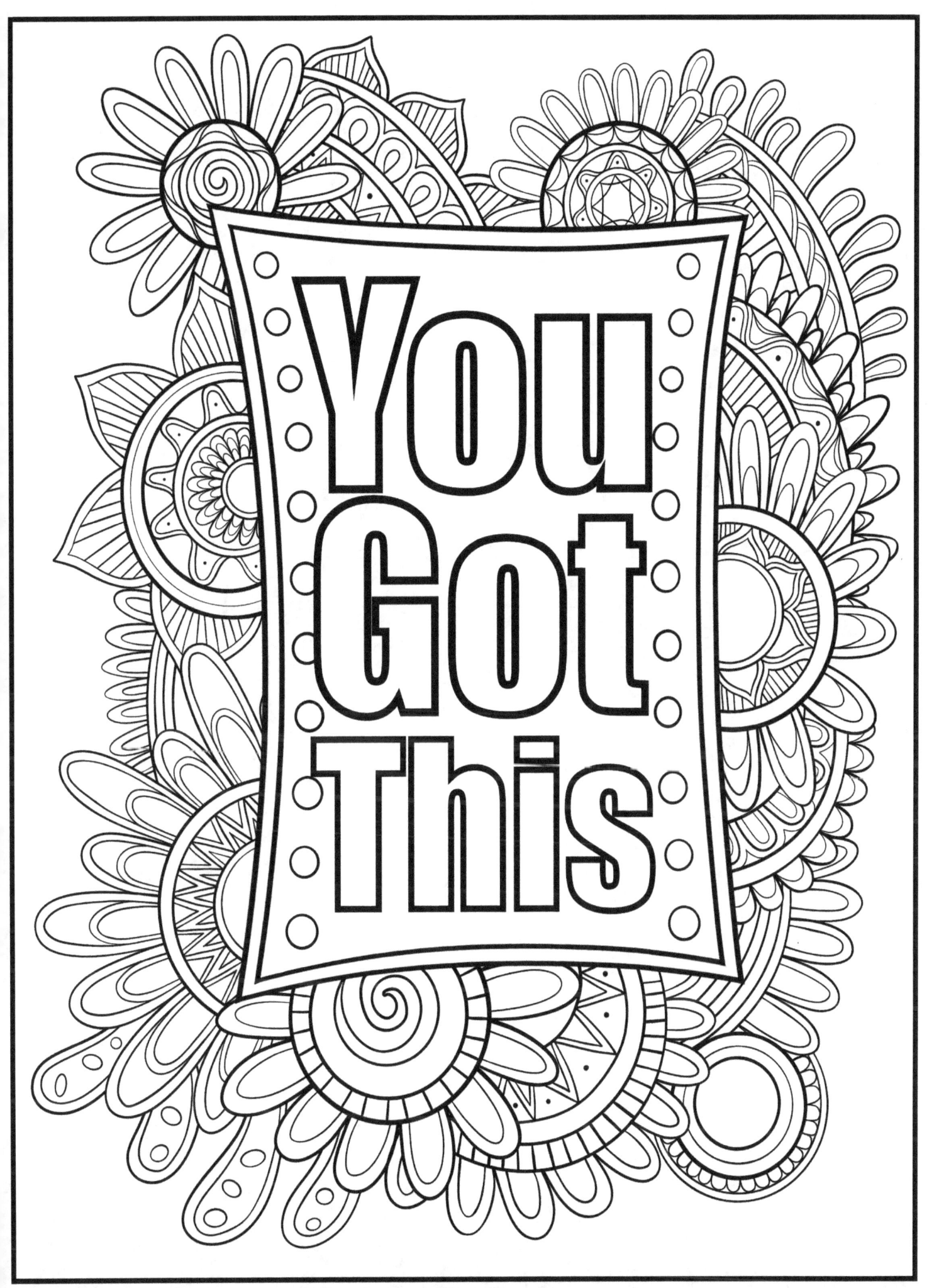

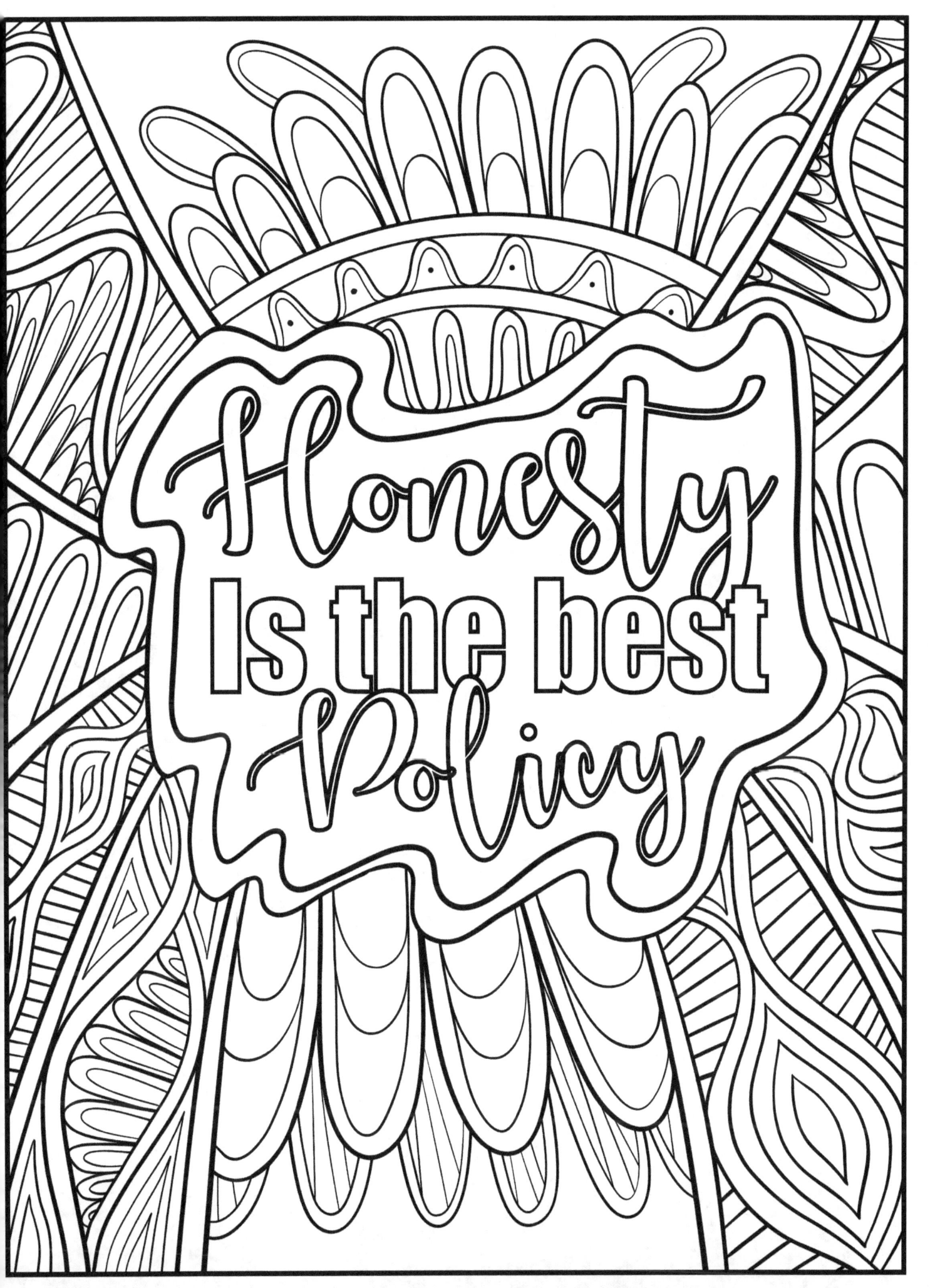

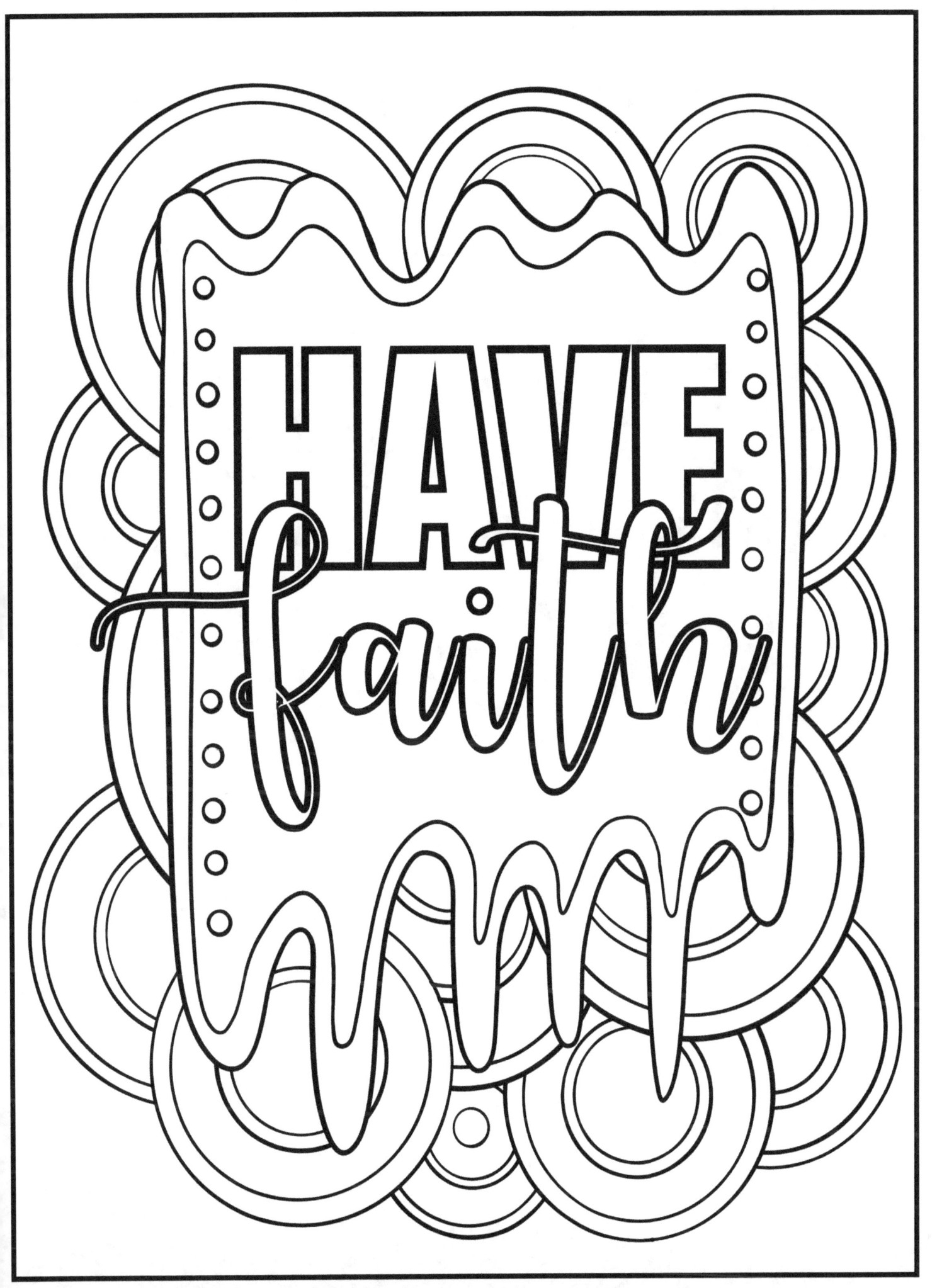

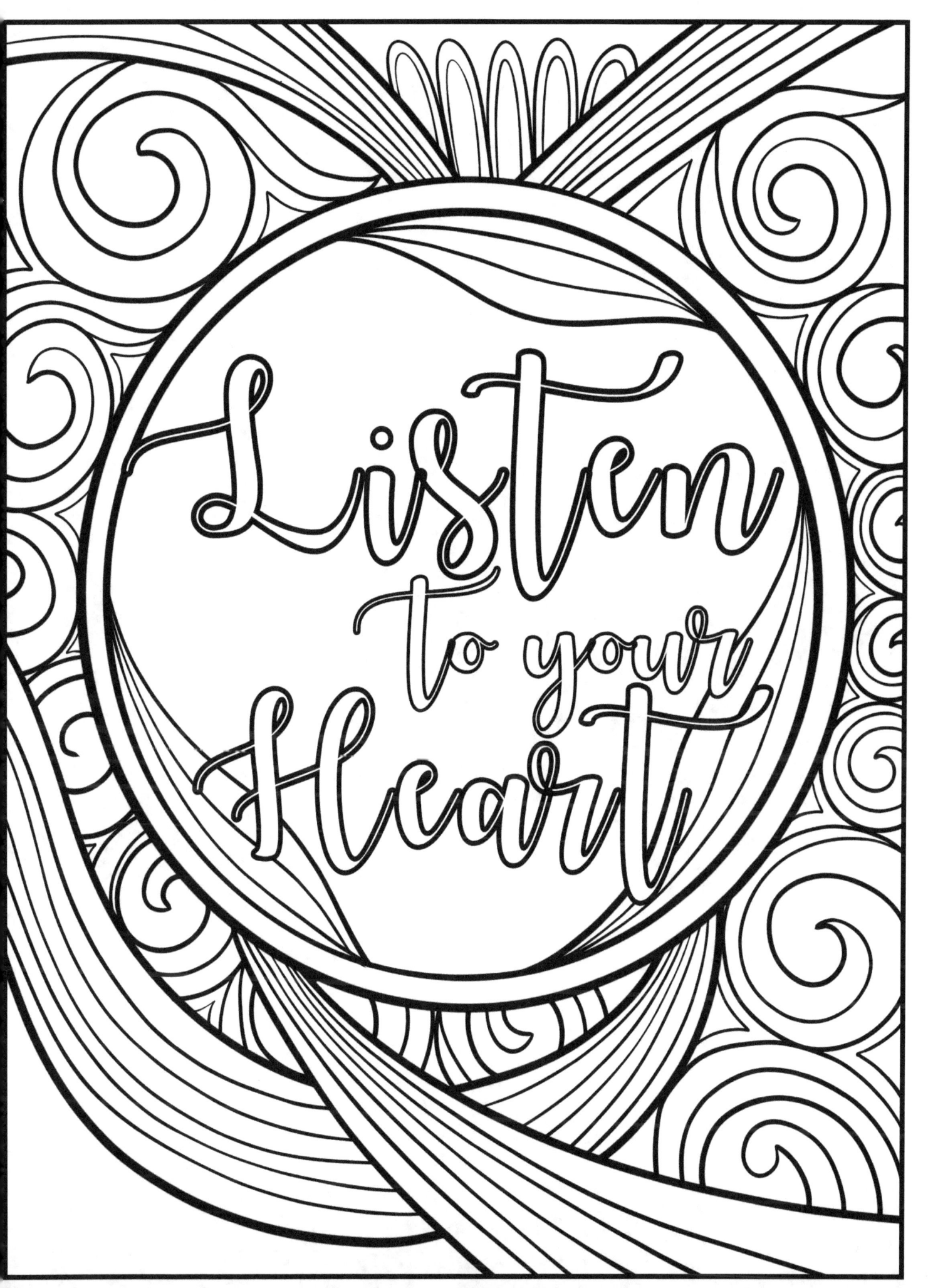

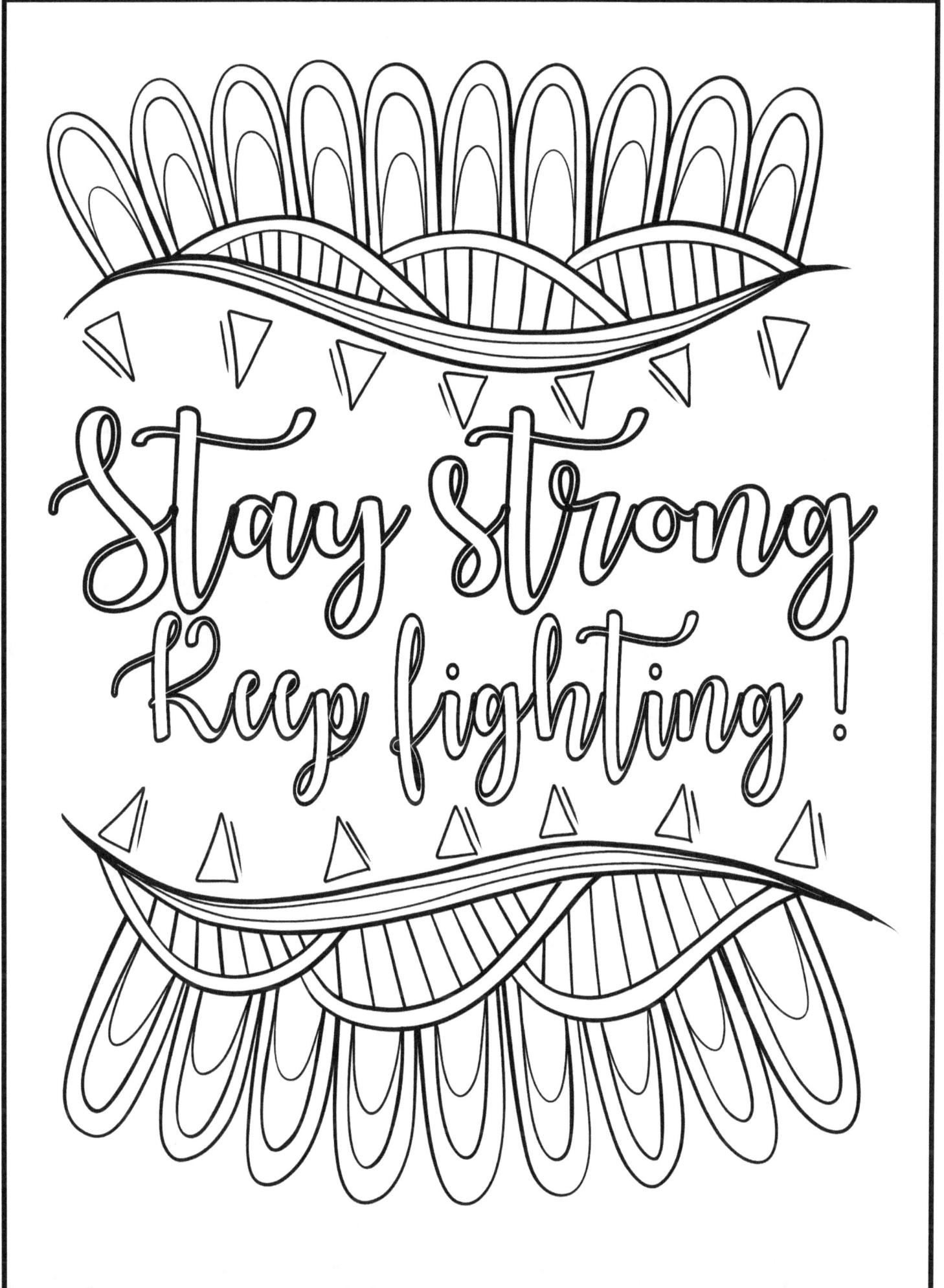

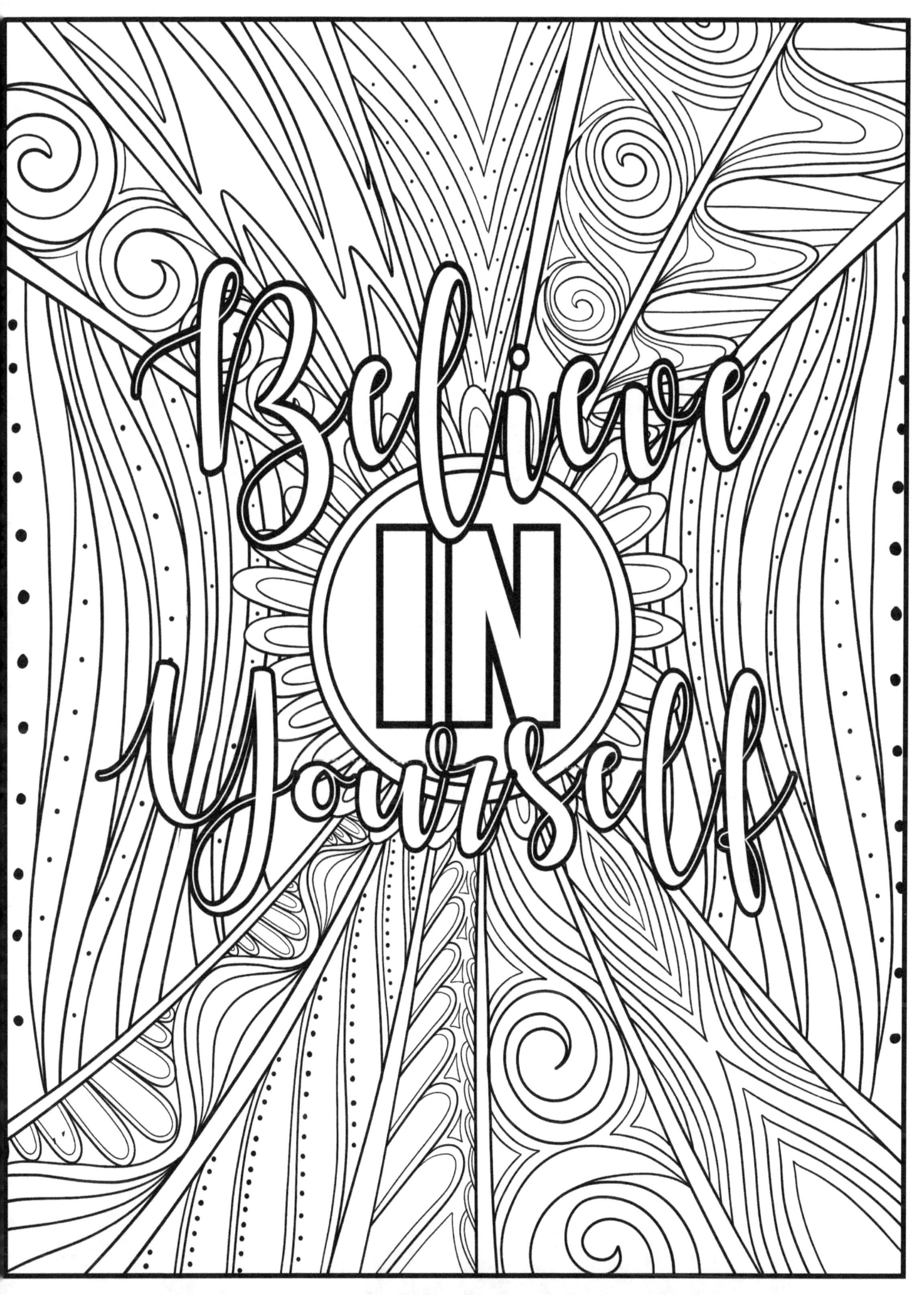

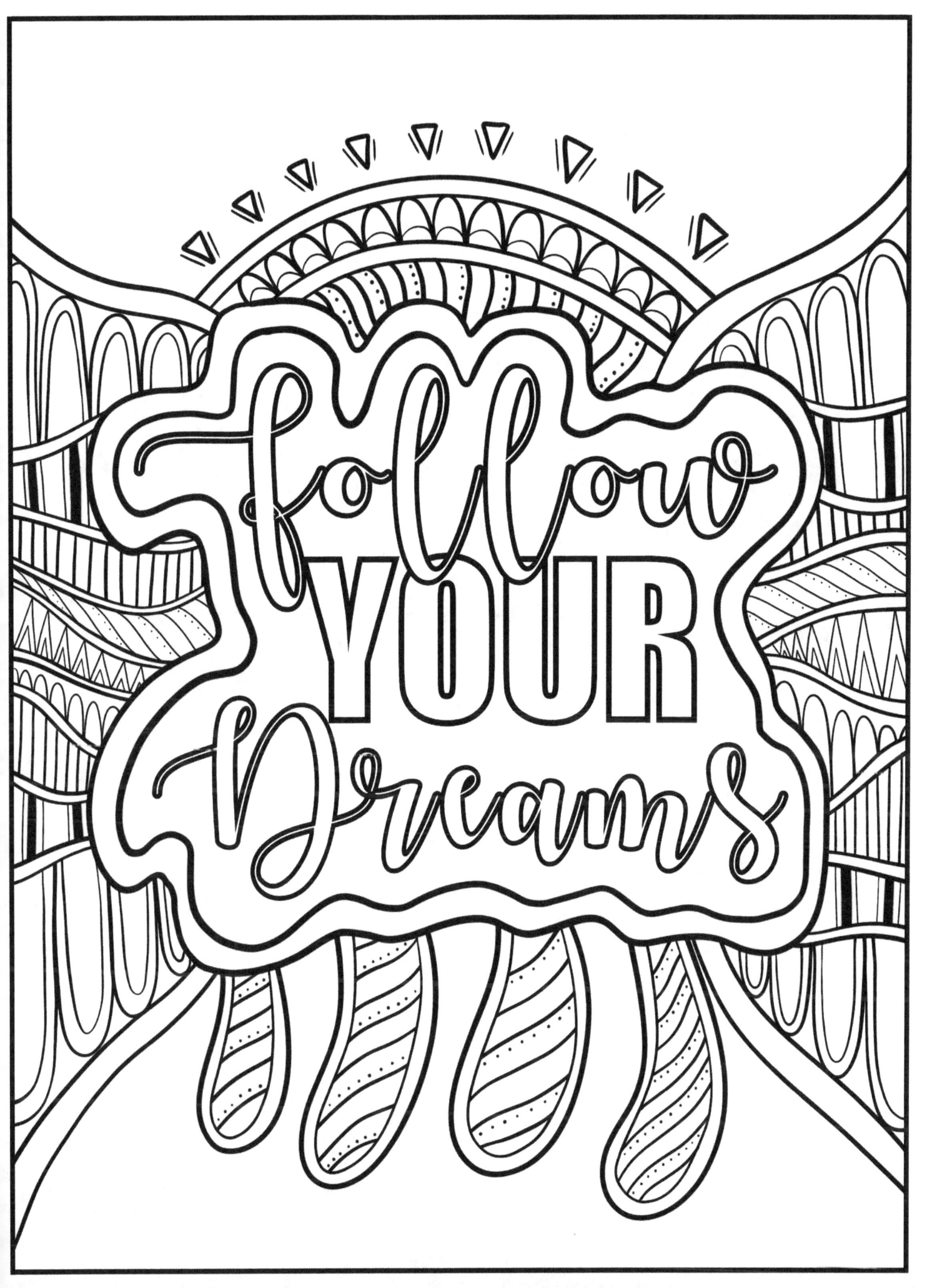

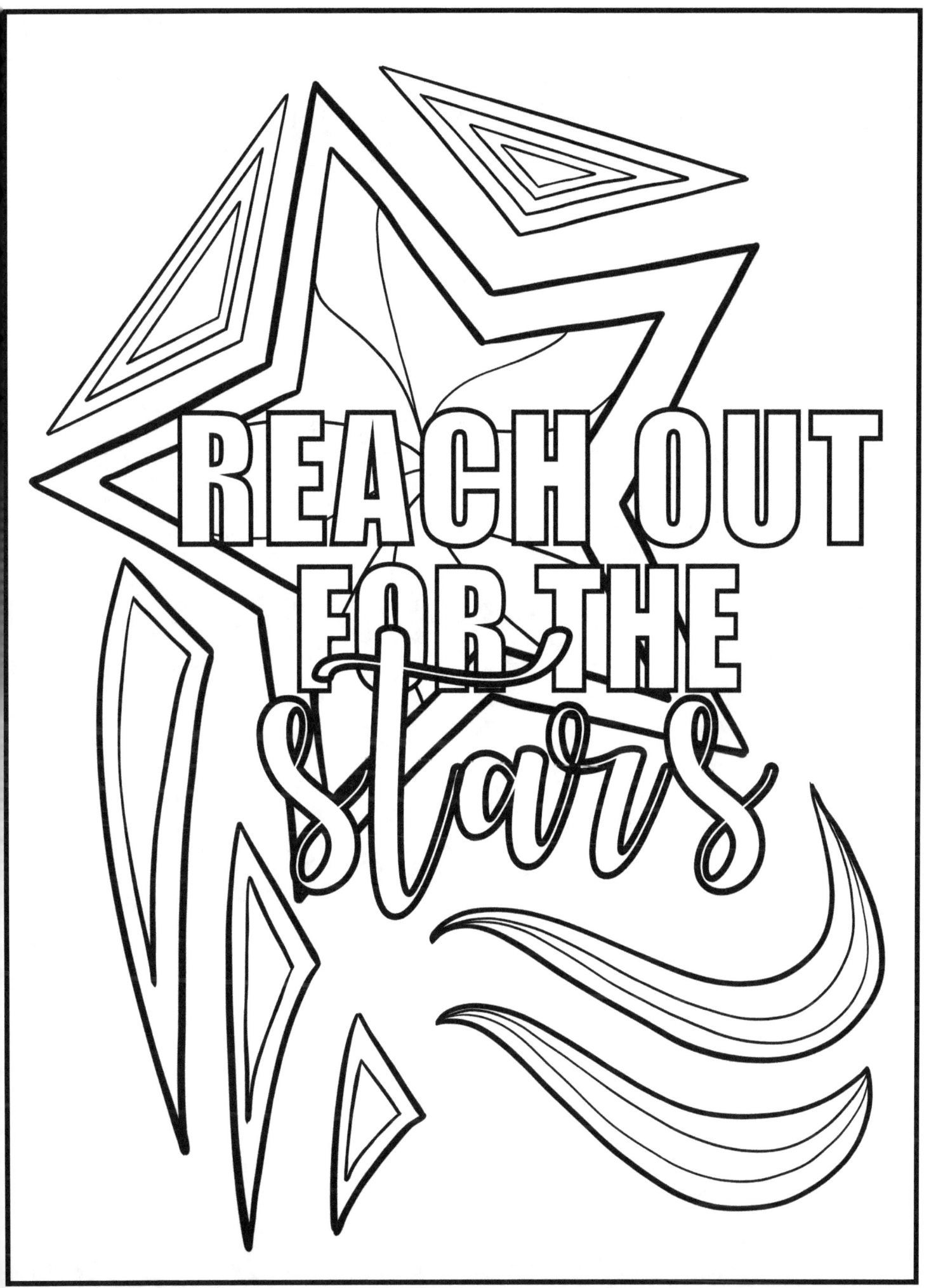

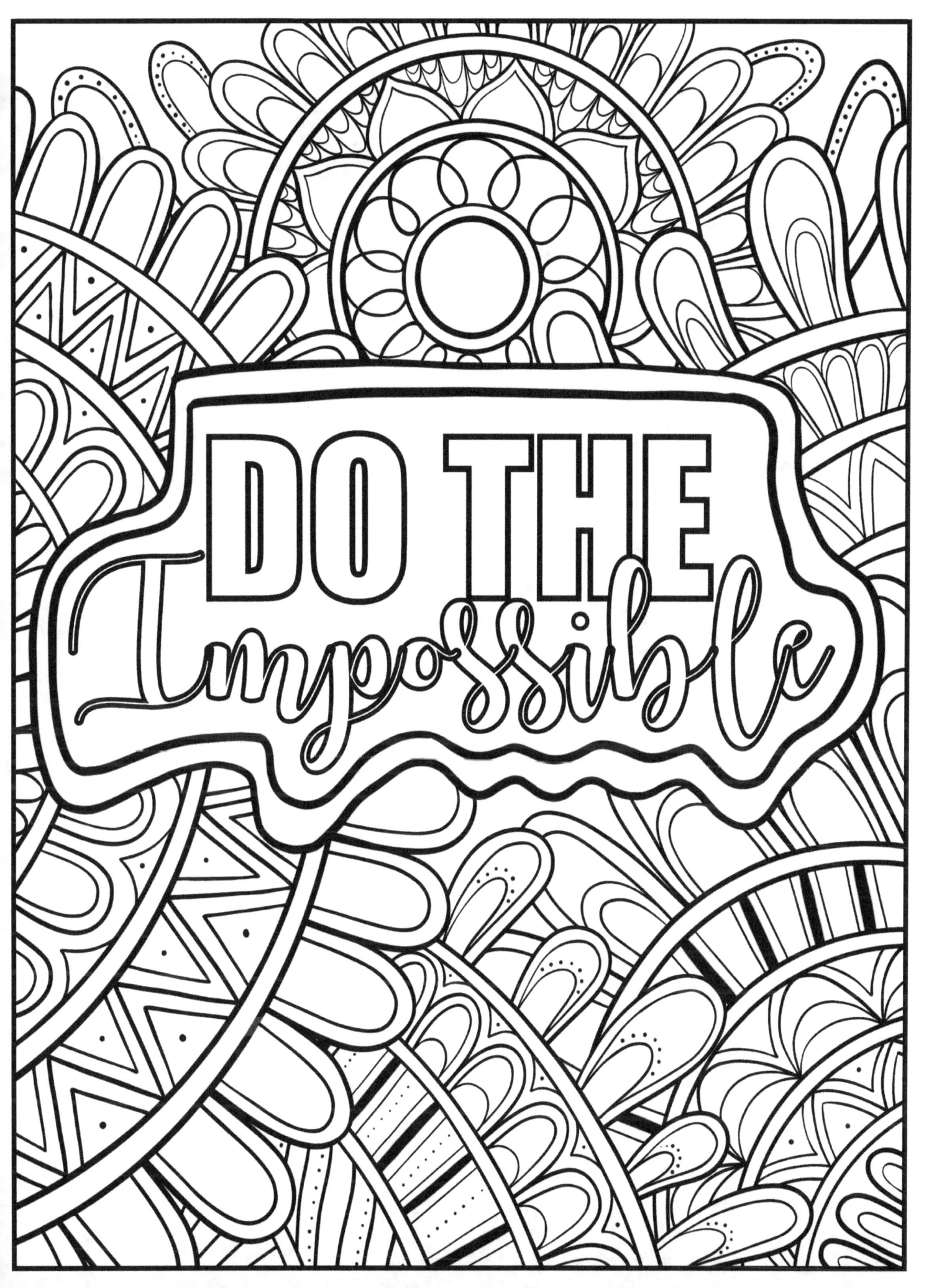

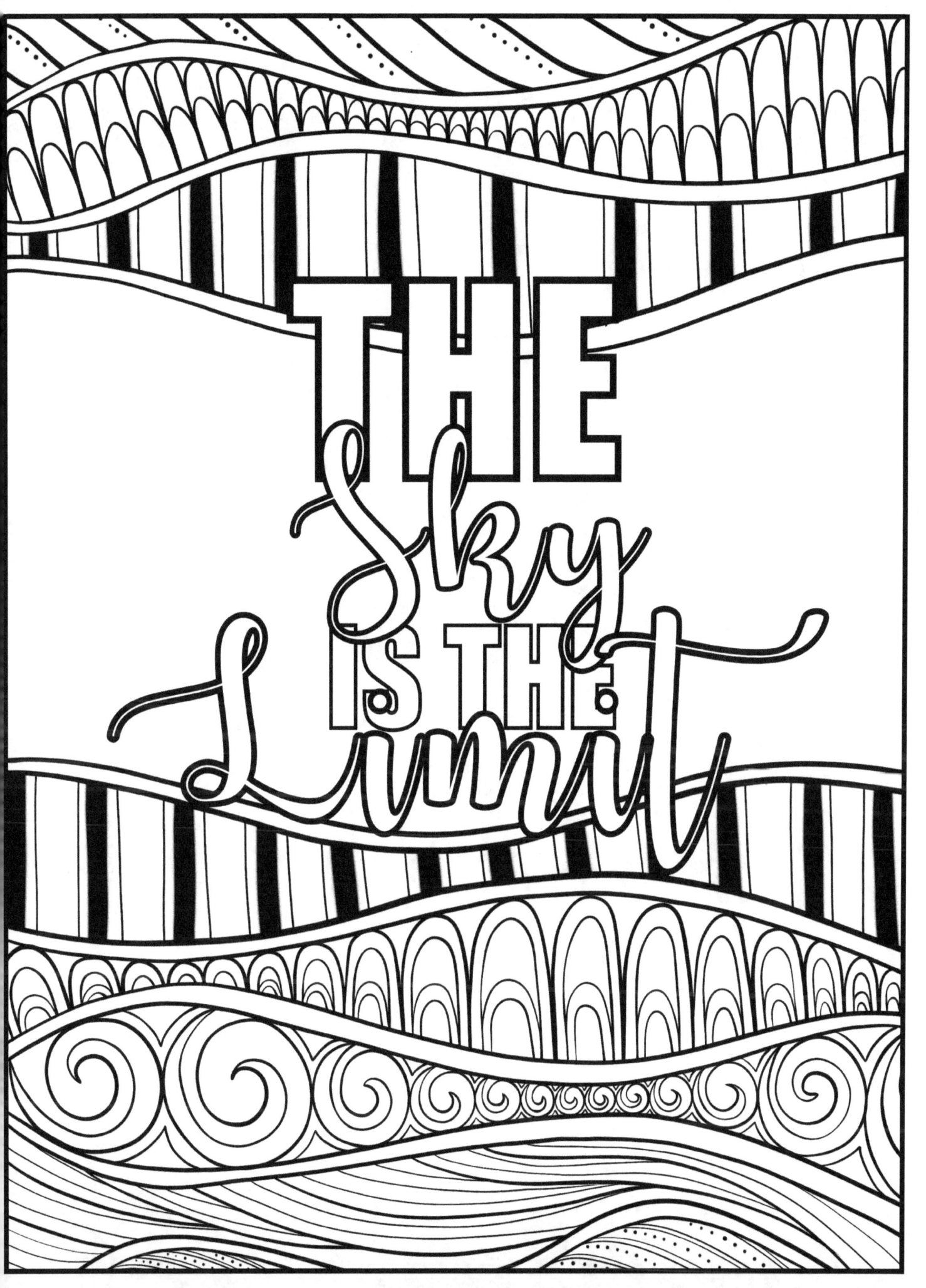

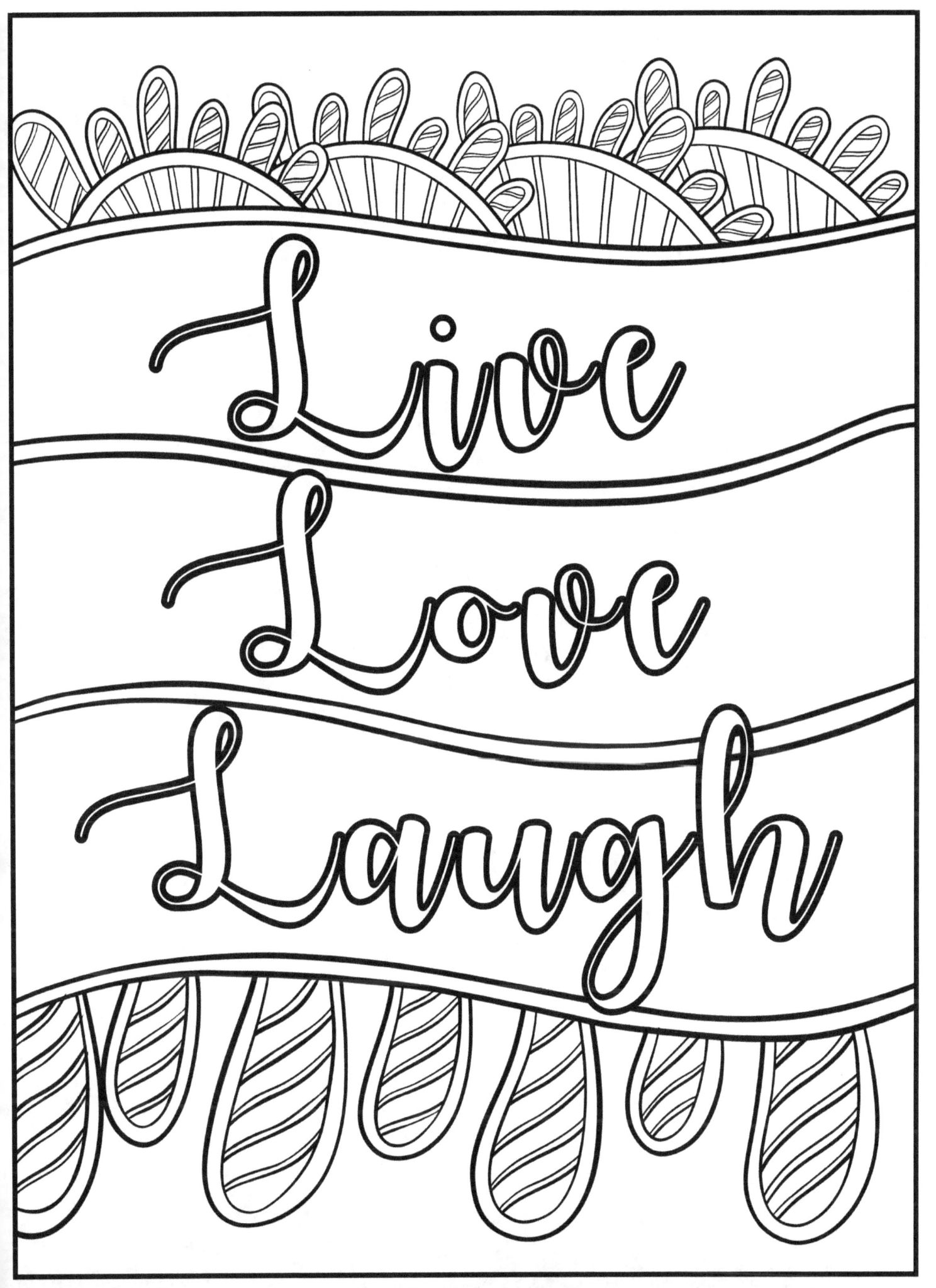

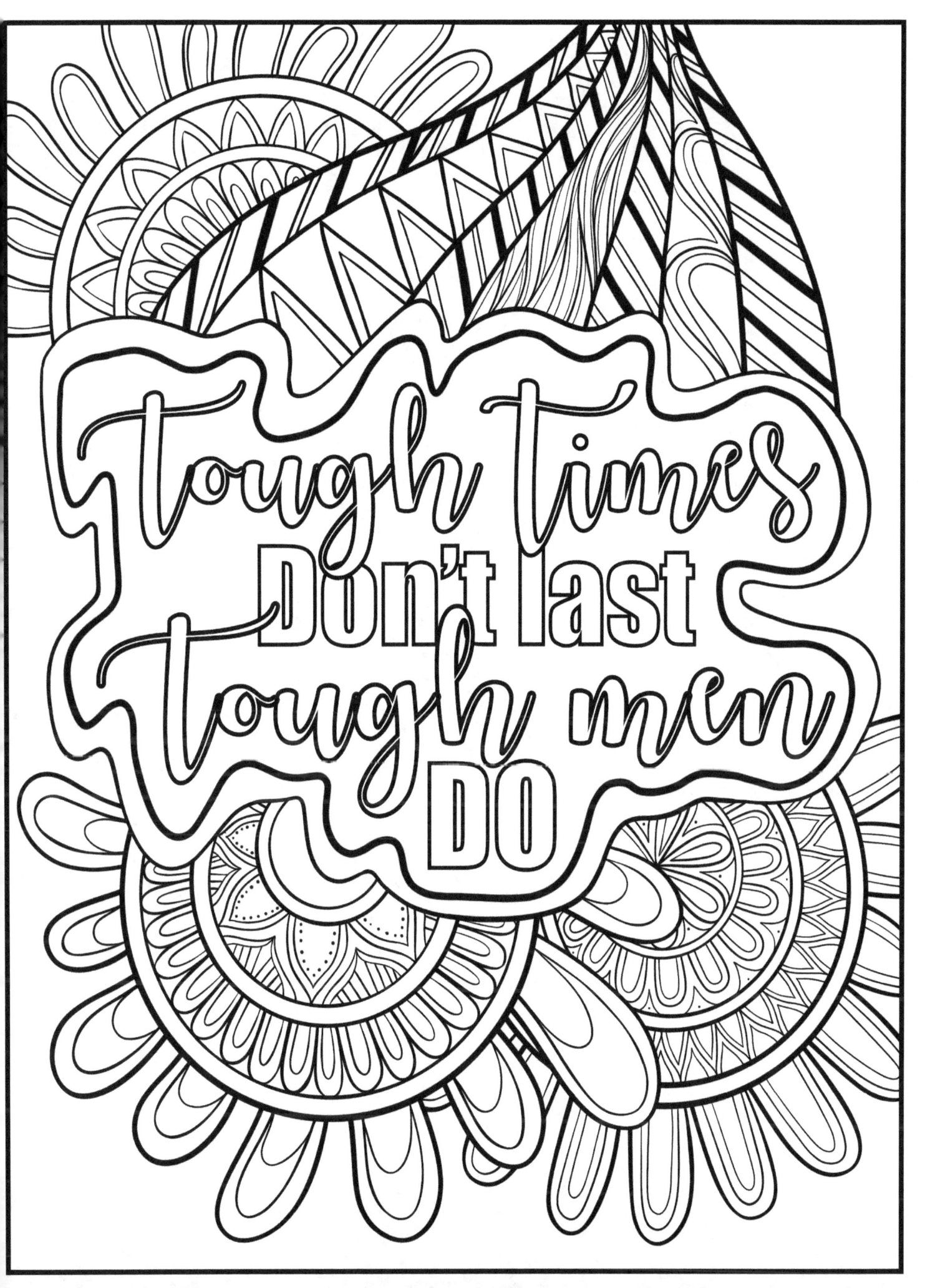

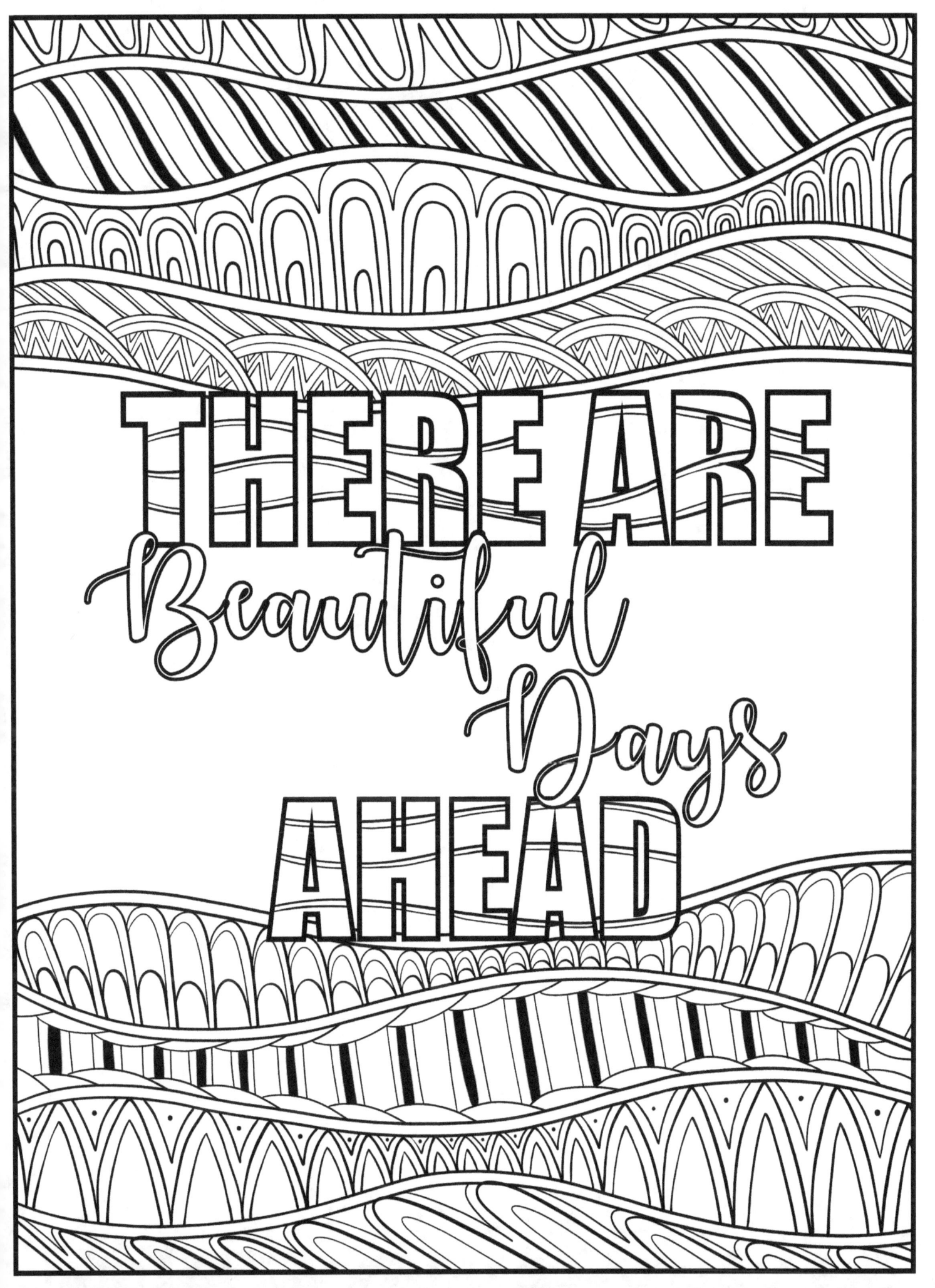

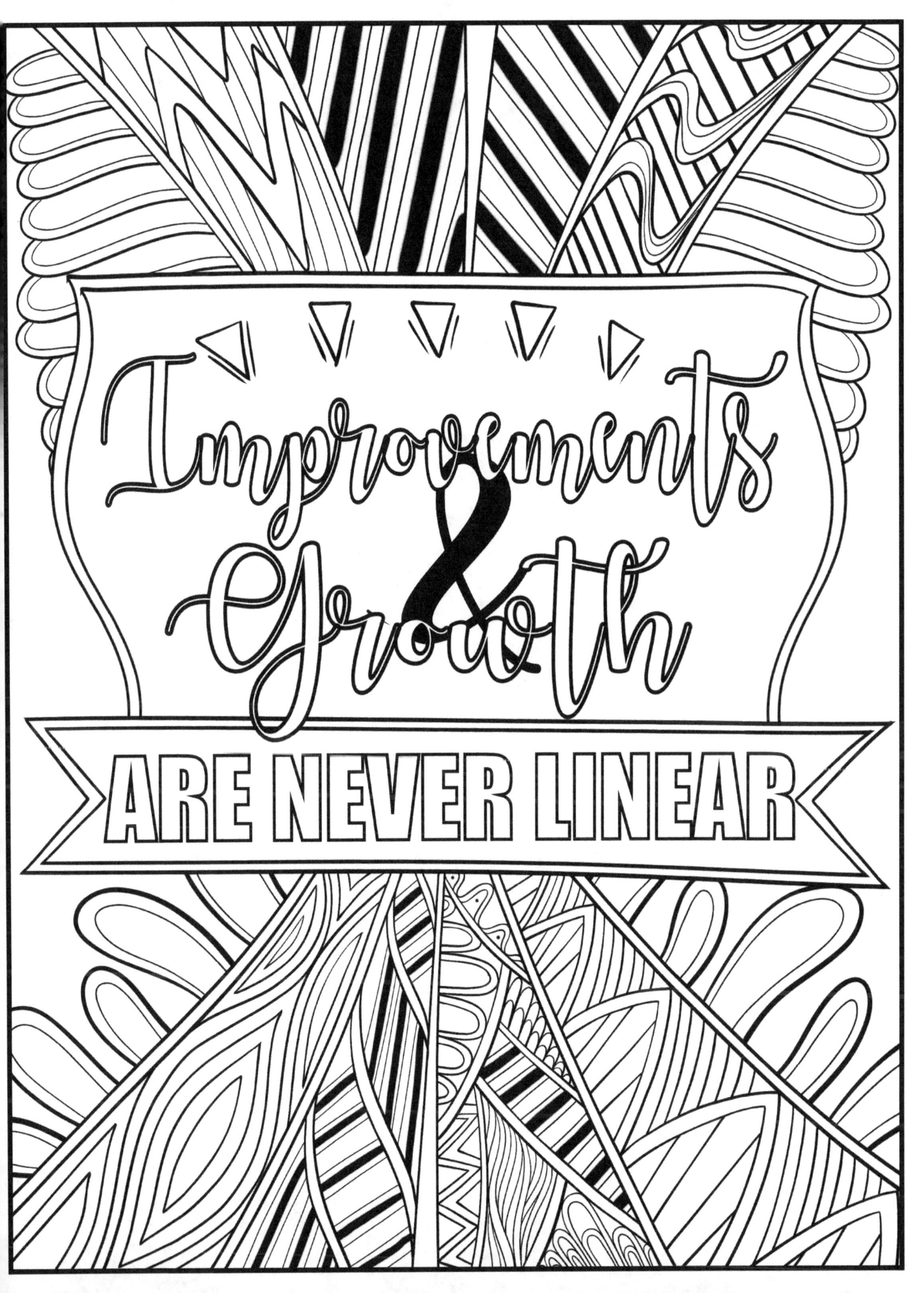

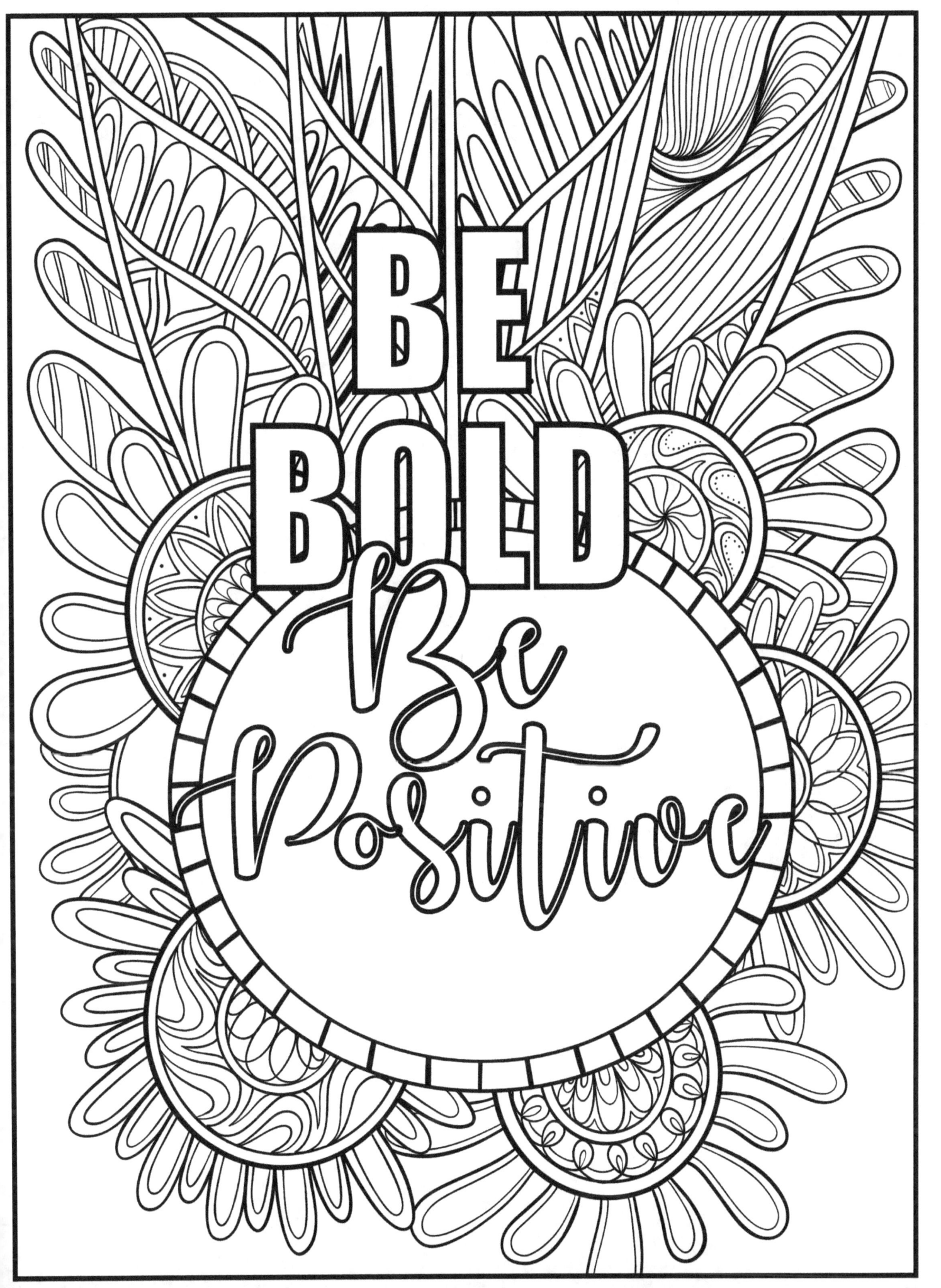

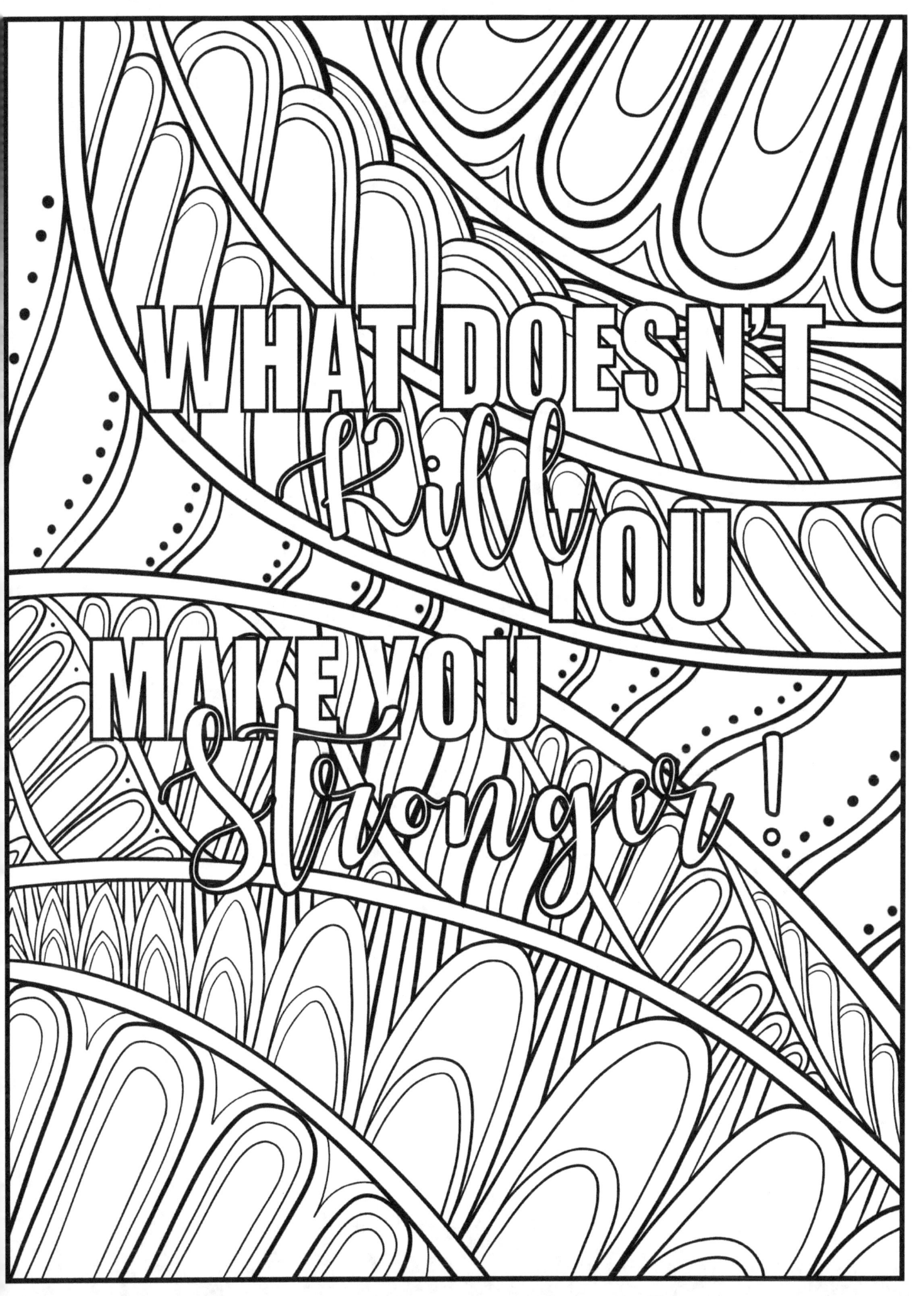

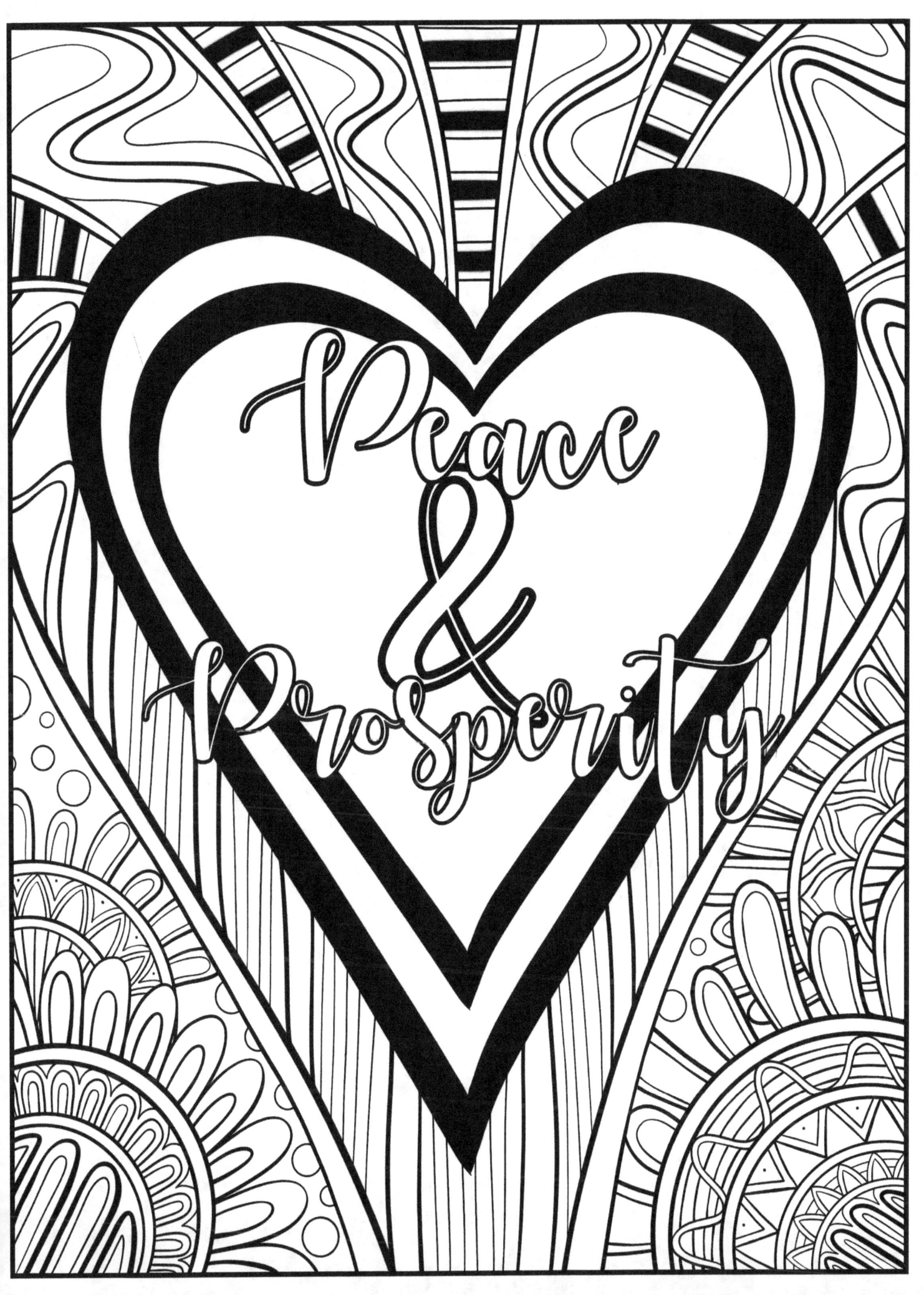

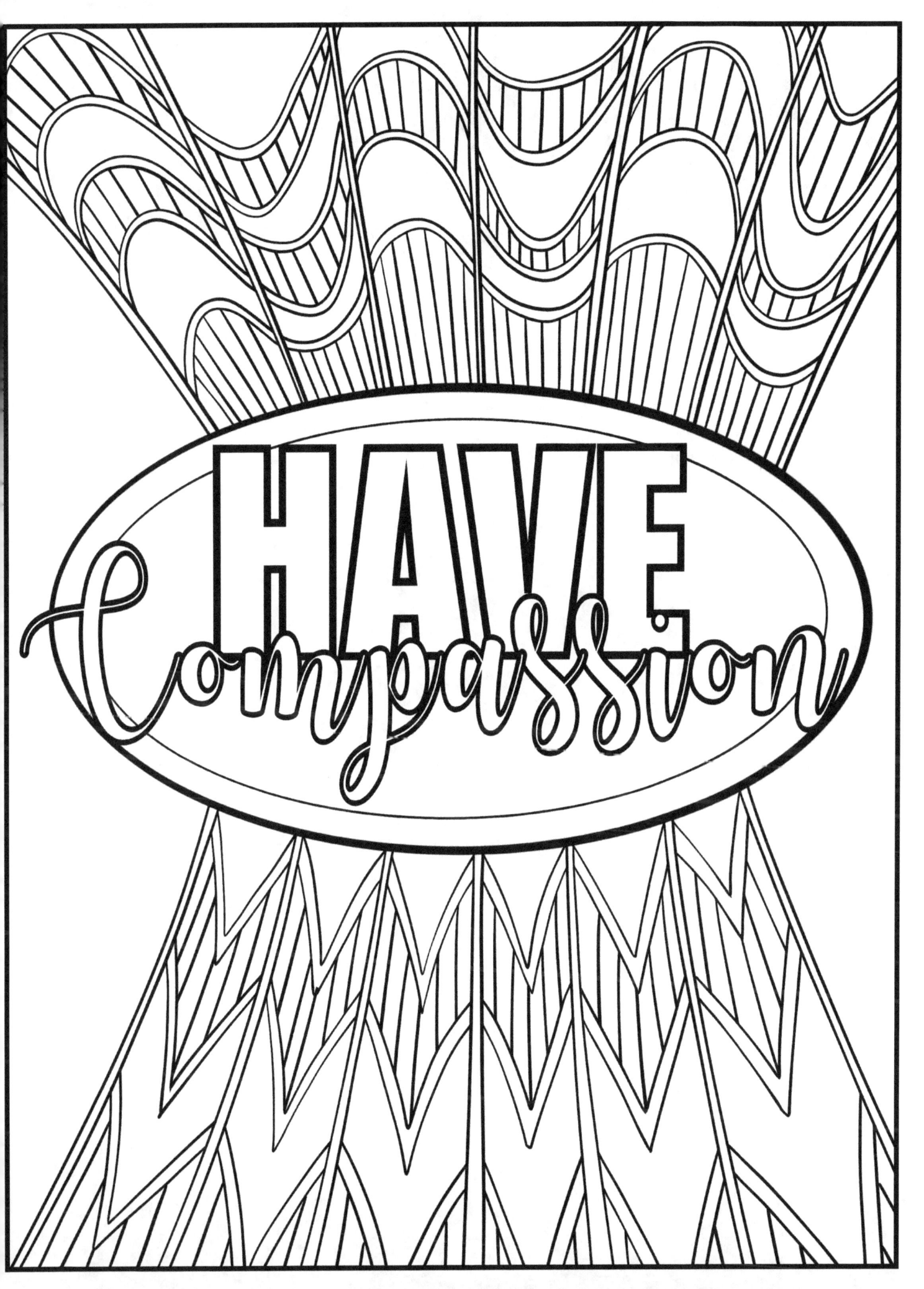

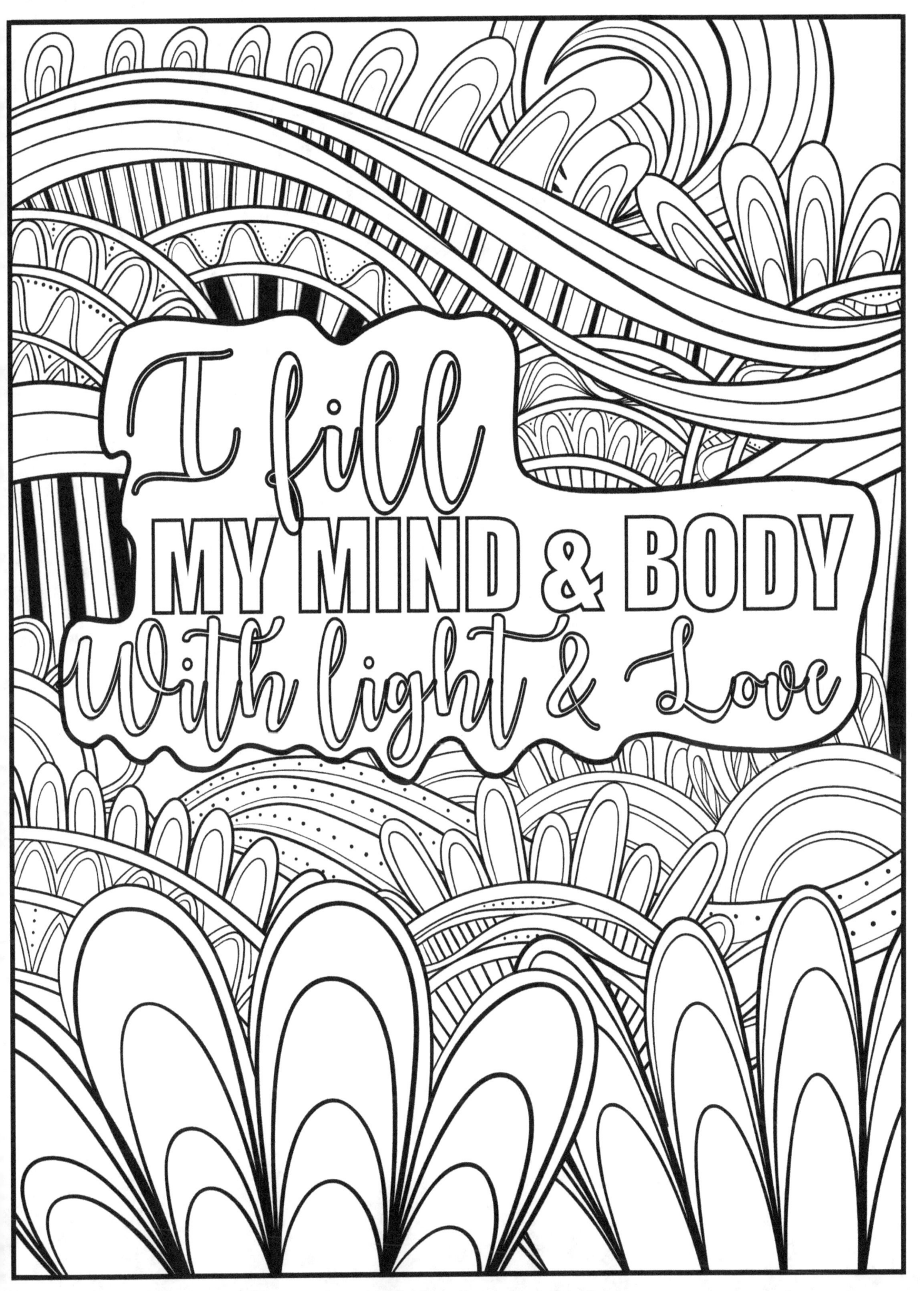

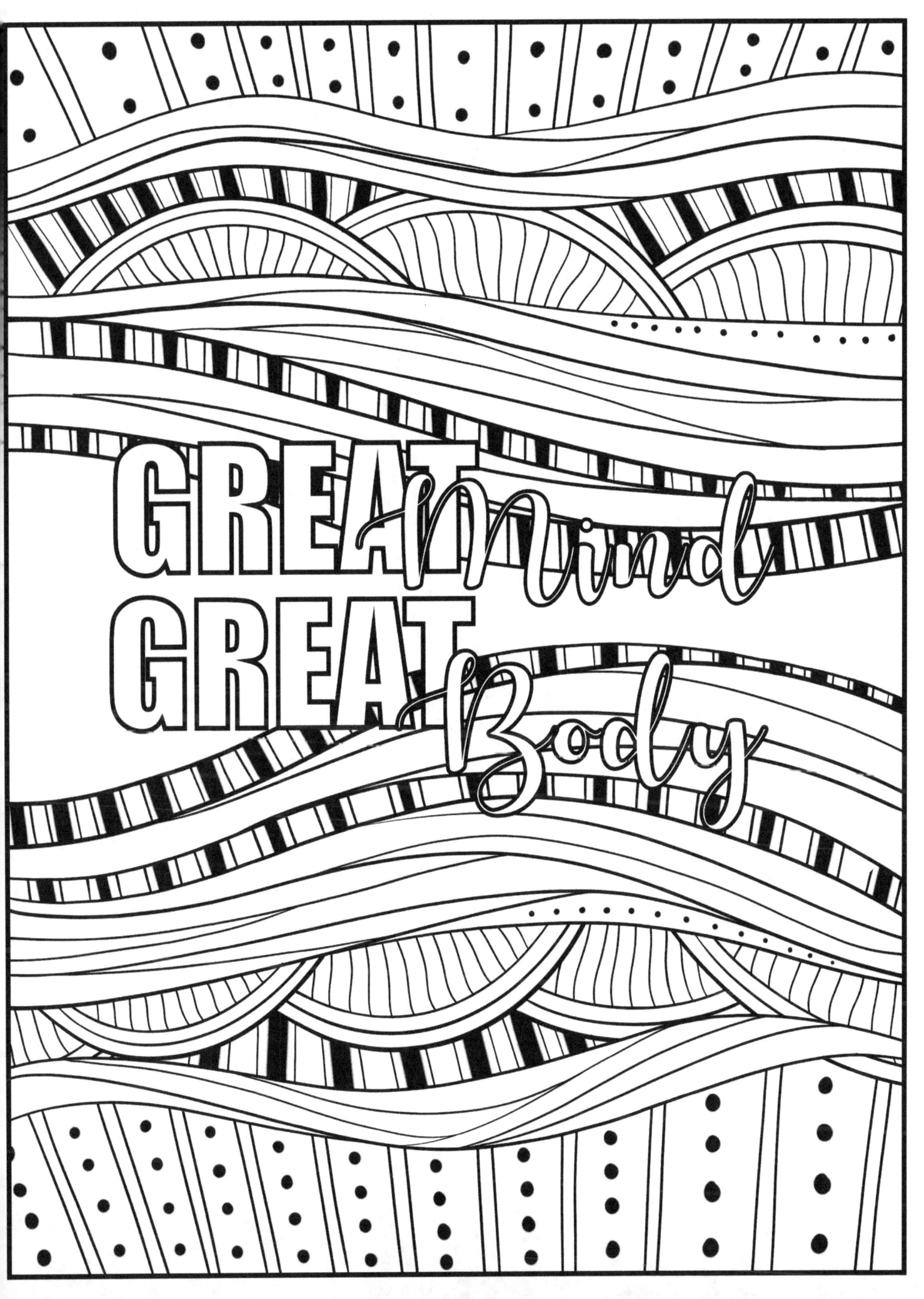

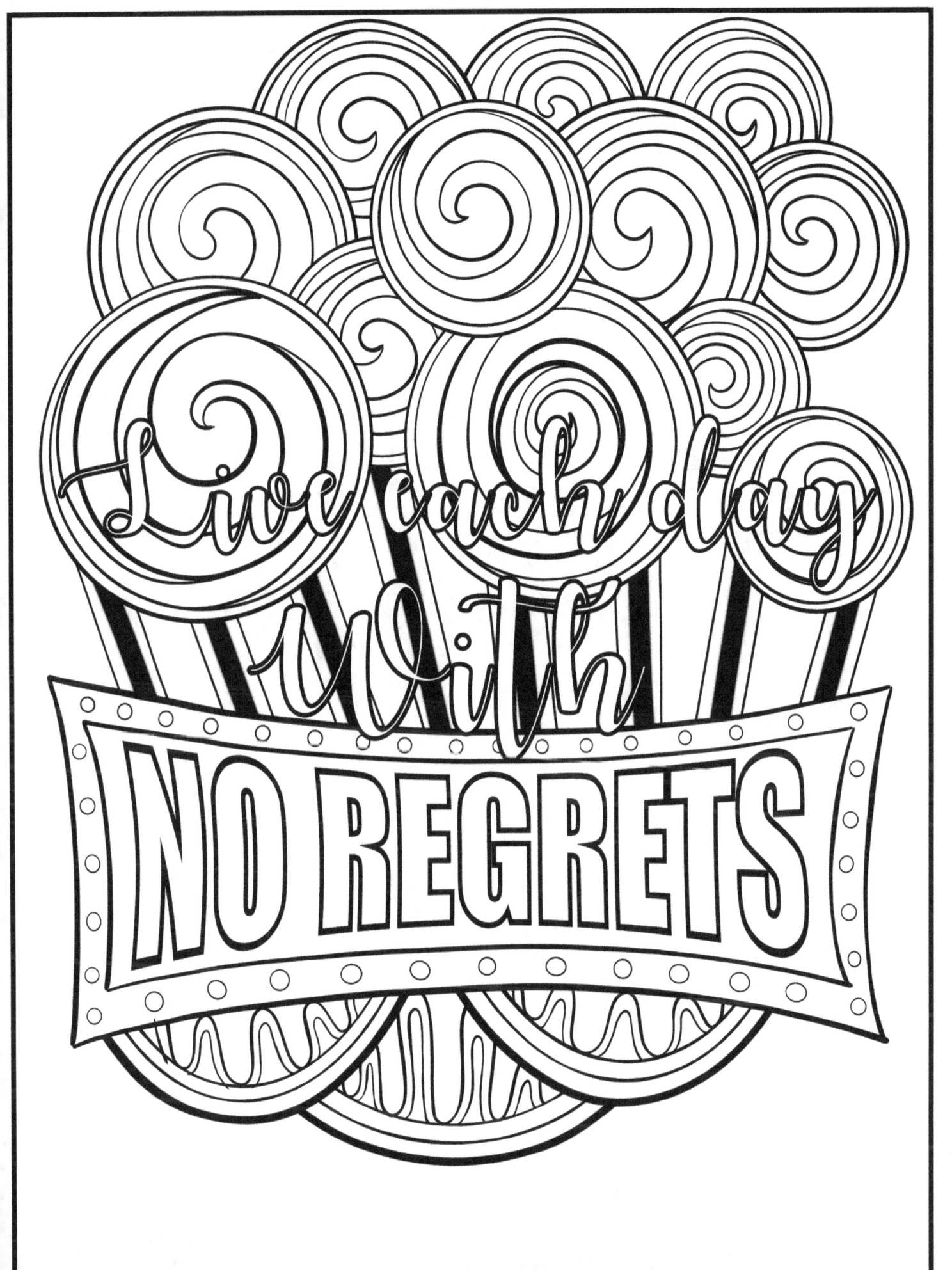

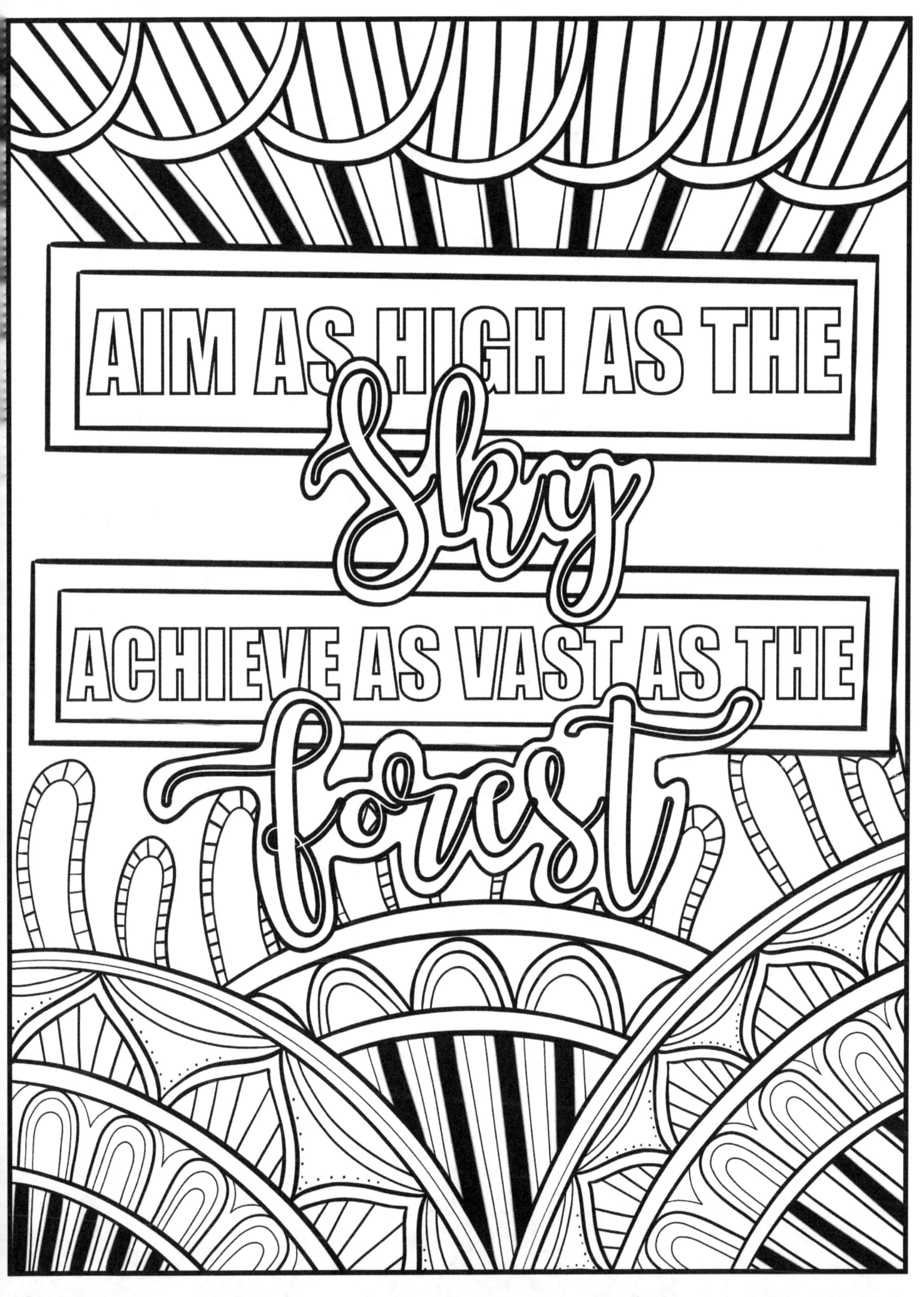

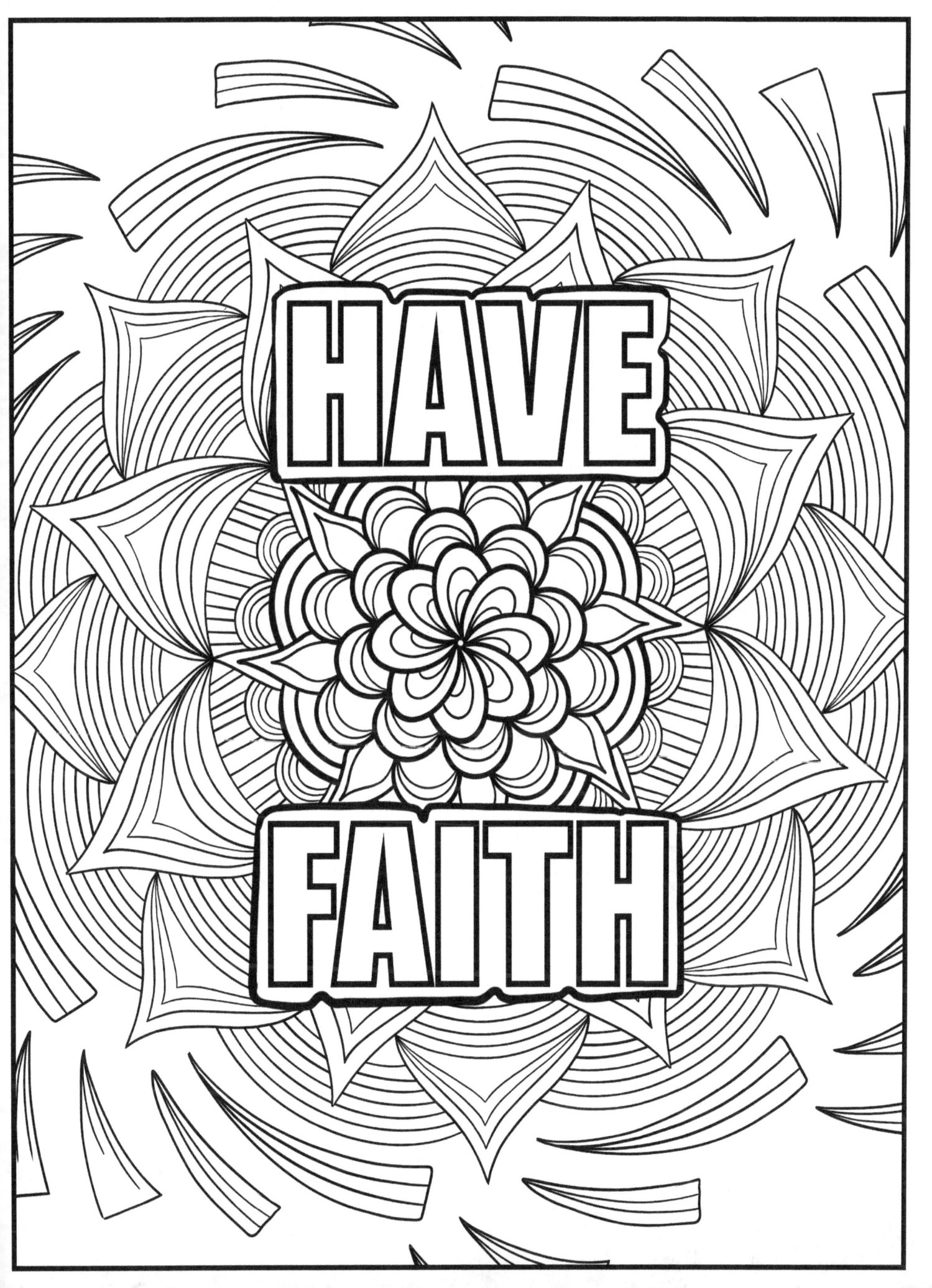